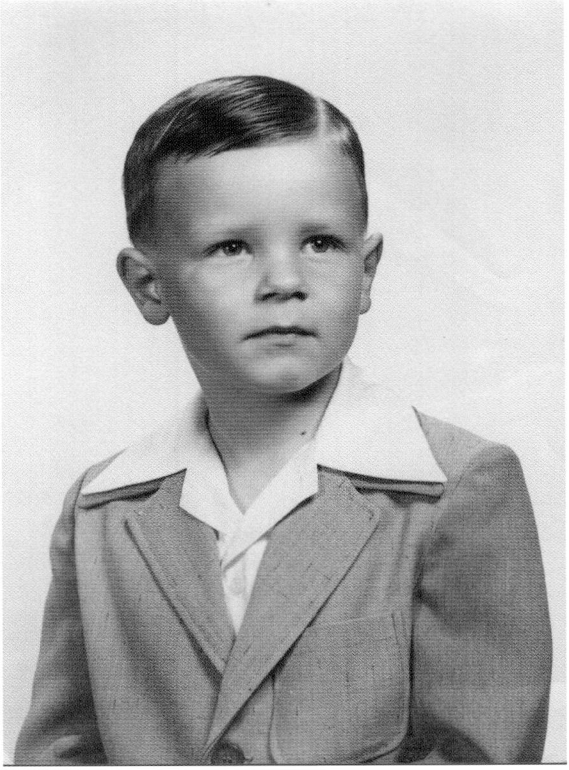

Growing Up Bookish

Growing Up Bookish

An Anglo-American Memoir

Richard Wendorf

OAK KNOLL PRESS

2017

Published by
Oak Knoll Press
310 Delaware Street
New Castle, DE 19720

ISBN: 978-1-58456-358-7

© 2017 Richard Wendorf. All rights reserved.

Typesetting & design: Scott Vile at the Ascensius Press.

No part of this book may be reproduced without the express written consent of the publisher, except in cases of brief excerpts in critical reviews and articles. All inquiries should be addressed to Oak Knoll Press, 310 Delaware Street, New Castle, DE 19720.

Printed in the Czech Republic on acid-free paper meeting the requirements of ANSI/NISO Z39.48.1992 (Permanence of Paper)

Library of Congress Cataloging-in-Publication Data
Names: Wendorf, Richard, author.
Title: Growing up bookish : an Anglo-American memoir / Richard Wendorf.
Description: First edition. | New Castle, Delaware : Oak Knoll Press, 2016. | Includes index.
Identifiers: LCCN 2016041012 | ISBN 9781584563587 (acid-free paper)
Subjects: LCSH: Wendorf, Richard. | Americans--England--Biography. | Scholars--Biography. | Museum directors--England--Bath--Biography. | Library directors--Massachusetts--Boston--Biography. | Art historians--Biography. | Critics--Biography.
Classification: LCC CT275.W387185 A3 2016 | DDC 818/.603 [B] --dc23 LC record available at https://lccn.loc.gov/2016041012

In Memoriam

Harold and Jeanne

Maurine and Frank

Dick, Carol, and Rex

Clay, Giff, Larry, and Charles

John, Graham, David, David, and Rachel

Charles, Grace, Mary, and Jack

Bing, Earl, and Barry

Jean and Ruth

Hugh, Bill, Rodney, Elli, and James

Arthur, Bill, and Jean

Stan, Michael, Franny, Ruth, and Richard

Arthur and Charlotte

The publication of this book has been generously supported by members of the Claverton Theatre Club

Table of Contents

Preface	1
Chapter One: *In the Heart of the Heart of the Country*	3
Chapter Two: *Teaching Is What It Was All About*	20
Chapter Three: *(Yet Another) Yank At Oxford*	33
Chapter Four: *As Ever, Charles*	48
Chapter Five: *An Inconvenient Revelation*	61
Chapter Six: *Living With Piranesi*	73
Chapter Seven: *The Petrified Mouse*	90
Chapter Eight: *Self-Portrait With Donors*	104
Chapter Nine: *Libraries, Museums — and Me*	117
Chapter Ten: *Highly Skilled Migrant*	132
Chapter Eleven: *Good Taste Costs No More*	143
Chapter Twelve: *Sitting for One's Picture*	166
Acknowledgements *(And Other Conundrums)*	185
Credits for Images	187
Index	189

Even just the bewildering minute counts; you have to give yourself up, and then recover yourself, and the third moment is having something to say, before you have wholly forgotten both surrender and recovery. Of course the self recovered is never the same as the self before it was given.

T. S. Eliot to Stephen Spender

What shall we call our "self"? Where does it begin? Where does it end? It overflows into everything that belongs to us — and then it flows back again. I know a large part of myself is in the clothes I choose to wear. I've got a great respect for *things*! One's self — for other people — is one's expression of one's self; and one's house, one's furniture, one's garments, the books one reads, the company one keeps — these things are all expressive.

Madame Merle, in Henry James's *Portrait of a Lady*

PREFACE

The world into which I was born contained few books, few readers, and almost no writers. I shall eventually expire surrounded by thousands of books, most of which I have read, a few of which I have written, and more than a few (I imagine) that I shall leave sadly untouched behind me. As the dying Clive James remarked, "If you don't know the exact moment when the lights will go out, you might as well read until they do."

This memoir attempts to make sense of the contours of a life surrounded by, embedded in, and attempting to nourish the world of books and libraries. And because I have also devoted part of my professional life to art history and to the museum world, I have also written about the transitions I've made between these two spheres. I have not attempted to integrate my intellectual growth with every other aspect of my life — difficult and messy (and unconvincing) as most such attempts usually are. This is a memoir, not a full autobiography. I have recognized my children and my partners, but they are not at the center of this narrative. Nor do I seek to settle old scores or judge my various colleagues. As a teacher, as a dean, and as the director of three institutions, I have become closely acquainted with human error and human frailty, but I have always embraced Paul Ricoeur's "hermeneutics of faith" rather than his "hermeneutics of suspicion." And I remain, perhaps because of my upbringing, an optimistic person, with a glass more than half full. In my view, if you're not an optimist, you have no business running a cultural institution in the first place.

In the chapters that follow, I focus on a series of defining moments and environments that have made my career as a scholar and as a library and museum director possible. In my scholarly work I have referred to such moments as "pressure points" and I have referred to such environments as examples of the "habitus" (in Pierre Bourdieu's recent coinage): the cultural and social spheres that leave their lasting imprint upon us. Perhaps because of these various forces, my

Richard Wendorf

career has been somewhat unpredictable. I first intended to become a lawyer — and even reserved my place at Harvard Law School — but Williams sent me to Oxford and Oxford changed all that. I went to Princeton because the connection with Oxford was very strong and because I wanted to work within another small graduate program. Had I flown out to Stanford instead, I wonder how differently things might have turned out (probably not that differently at all). I didn't intend to return to the Midwest, to become an academic dean, to become an art historian, to become a library director, to leave Harvard for the Boston Athenæum, or to move to England to become a museum director. But professional patterns can be just as complicated and asymmetrical as personal ones, and I now find myself giving shape to a book on printing history that is based on unanswered questions in my doctoral dissertation forty years ago.

I begin this narrative by exploring the habitus of Cedar Rapids, Iowa, where I spent the first eighteen years of my life. This first essay — and those that follow — are meant to be read on their own terms, but taken together they should also, I hope, furnish some sense of the trajectory of my life and my career as I head towards my encounter with the proverbial three score and ten.

CHAPTER ONE

In the Heart of the Heart of the Country

I

I WAS BORN, at mid-century, in the middle of America's heartland. Several states could make a reasonable claim to that distinction — Missouri, Nebraska, perhaps even Kansas — but Iowans are rightfully proud of their geographical heritage and of the culture that has evolved there. Iowa is where the homesick Dvořák wrote some of his haunting Slavonic music, where Grant Wood painted almost all of his pictures, where Meredith Willson placed that most mid-American of American confections, *The Music Man*. And Cedar Rapids, where I was born and raised, lies at the heart of America's heartland.

My hometown is not as large as the state capital (Des Moines); it straddles the Cedar River rather than flanking the Mississippi; it boasts some small colleges but none of the state's three major universities. What it did have, when my family lived there, was a genuine sense of cohesion, of various cultural and commercial interests being of just about the right size, with neither a large university nor a state capitol casting an exaggerated shadow. My mother was born there, as was her mother. My father was a Chicagoan who rode a music scholarship to the small liberal arts college in my mother's hometown, met her while they both worked at the felicitously named Inter-Ocean Reinsurance Company, married her, and began his career there. It could have been otherwise.

Although he would rarely talk about it, my father had had what used to be called "a good war." A perforated eardrum prevented him from attending officers' candidate school in the Navy at the beginning of the conflict, but he dutifully enlisted in the Army as a private and made the long journey on foot and by thumb from the sole of the boot of Italy to the prisoner-of-war and concentration camps in Germany, which he helped to liberate. He fought in the Vosges Mountains (where he was wounded) and was generously promoted and decorated throughout the war. He was particularly proud of a beautiful medal from the Polish government, although my brother and I always maintained that a certain Polish count had taken a fancy to the handsome young man who could still play a mean clarinet. At the end of his tour of duty he was offered a captaincy and a position on Eisenhower's staff at SHAEF headquarters in Paris. He turned the offer down in order to return home — and, as he liked to say to me, "to have *you*."

I have often wondered how different my life might have been had my father summoned my mother to Paris and begun his marriage with her there. I would have been bilingual; I would have grown up with French food, French wine, French music, French theatre. I might have been that small boy in the photograph with a long baguette in his arms and a dark beret on his head. I would have lost my virginity at a very early age. I would have been cosmopolitan. I would have become an incessant talker, a political activist, a budding intellectual. I would not, in any form or manner, have been provincial.

But I was born and raised in the heart of the heart of my own country, and for that I remain thankful. I became, among many other things, well grounded. I knew that I had the unfailing support of my parents and a keen sense of where their boundaries lay. And their boundaries became mine. I knew where I stood — and I knew where other people stood. My parents did not have any deeply felt prejudices about race or religion or ethnicity and they shared a clear sense of duty, of fairness, and of appropriate behavior. They could be judgmental, even stern. My mother's most trenchant comment — one that she shared with her sister Maurine — was directed towards men whom they judged to be lightweight or ineffectual: "He's certainly a weak sister, isn't he, sis?"

I never wanted to be a weak sister, but neither did I wish to be aggressive — let alone a bully. That was easily done. My parents implicitly preached a different form of behavior, which was a middle course — a third way, as we might say today. They did not bang on about the golden

In the Heart of the Heart of the Country

rule, but I always felt that it was part of our familial compact: do unto others as you would have them do unto you. Be polite, be respectful, try to see the other person's point of view, try to put yourself in their place and gain *their* respect. I would like to think that this form of behavior has served me well, both personally and professionally, but it can also lead to overly cautious behavior, a resistance to confrontation, a reluctance to make difficult decisions. These are inhibitions that my brother, Jim, and I successfully worked through and that my parents never quite did, sharing a tendency to be the passive victims of other peoples' thoughtlessness and carelessness rather than simply sticking up for themselves. They both described themselves as fatalists — a concept I ran away from as fast as I possibly could.

This is only to say, of course, that they were very much part of their community and of their time. Cedar Rapids, after the war and during the fifties and early sixties, was an immensely complacent environment in which to live. Everyone had made sacrifices during World War II. It was time to settle down, to focus on business and leisure, to begin to weave a new social fabric within one's family and among one's friends. My parents were very much part of this endeavor. My father, Harold, although not a native Cedar Rapidian (perhaps *because* he wasn't a native of the city), became an energetic "joiner" and striver: Rotary Club, the church, the Shriners, the Masons, the Jesters, the Chamber of Commerce, the annual cancer drive, the board of trustees of his alma mater, first one country club and then, with great pride and pleasure, the even grander one. He had arrived, although he didn't always feel fully accepted, respected, or appreciated.

My mother, Jeanne, was quite different. Her friends always referred to her as an elegant woman, a "real lady." She was, in fact, a quiet and even painfully shy person; her elegance was natural but it was also dictated by her innate cautiousness. She cleaned the house before her housekeeper arrived so that she wouldn't be the subject of gossip within the community; instead of saying that she didn't like something, she would simply say that it was "different" — and yet she could write a scalding letter when the opportunity arose, usually about corporate failings (those weak sisters once again). She never forsook her native manner of pronouncing various words: "Missoura" was located to the south of us, if you could find the right "rowt" to take you there; you "worshed" your hands; a creek was a "crick," a roof a "ruff." People were either "matour" or they weren't, and I certainly didn't want to be immatour.

Jeanne's family was English on both sides — Hamblin and Bromwell, the latter tribe arriving on the eastern shore of Maryland in the early eighteenth century — whereas my father's family was half Scottish and half German (Honeyman and Wendorf), with his cousins all marrying Italians in Chicago with exotic names like Maggio and Ferrari. Weekends with our cousins in Chicago were always eye-opening. I had never imagined that an entire family — let alone an Italian family — could live peacefully together in a cellar, but that's what one did during the summer before the introduction of air-conditioning, with the local produce vendors and ice men peddling their goods by the door that led to the alley behind the house.

What made our particular family different from others was the fact that, for the first ten years of my life, I had two mothers. My mother's sister was eight years older than she was. Maurine, whom we always referred to as Mimi, became an important fixture in the local high school, teaching music, working alongside Grant Wood (who taught art courses), and at one point teaching her own sister, an episode about which neither of them was ever very comfortable. Maurine was lively, headstrong, broad of beam, silver of hair, and fast heading towards spinsterhood. My parents invited her to live with us, which gives you some sense of how saintly my father could occasionally be. Harold and Jeanne had a built-in babysitter, Maurine had her two boys, and those two boys had the best of all worlds, playing not just one parent against the other but having recourse to Mimi when we couldn't otherwise get our way.

Maurine, for her part, was socially engaged in the community, an old-fashioned do-gooder. My father liked to say that each generation should do better than the one before, by which he meant material improvement. Maurine was more likely to ask us if we realized how fortunate we were. I especially remember her asking us if we would like to join her on Saturday mornings when she visited "the colored people." When we demurred, she would announce that her friend Billy Grapey would accompany her instead — and that, of course, generated enough jealousy to send us smartly into the back seat of her black and gray Plymouth.

Maurine seemed to know everyone, always had the right thing to say, always made sure that we shook hands, looked people in the eye, and thanked them for inviting us in. The day she announced that she was going to marry her old high-school sweetheart and move to Seattle was a sad day indeed. My brother looked at Francis Pressler across the dinner table and asked, "Are you the man who is taking our Mimi away from us?" But Maurine had chosen well, and Frank turned out to be a mentor of an entirely different sort — a champion swimmer, a skipper and water-skier, a hiker and camper, someone eager to immerse those two spoiled city boys in the natural world of the American Northwest.

Maurine's presence in our lives was especially important because we came from a very small family: my father was an only child and all four of my grandparents had died by the time I was one or two. My mother's first cousin, Jim Bromwell, had four children with his wife, Dorothy, and Max, Sissy, Cathy, and Jimmy became our close friends. This meant, among other things, that we shared Thanksgiving and Christmas dinners with them and with their other relatives, usually in the city but occasionally on a family farm where we would be allowed to run wild — but not to see the decapitation of a well-fed turkey. There would always be a grown-ups' table and a children's table, grace and gravy, scalloped oysters and mashed potatoes, leftovers for supper in the evening, and endless talk about far-distant aunts, uncles, and cousins with exotic names like Zula and Lura whom we would never meet, never know.

"Big Jim" Bromwell was the *pater familias* of this loving brood and an imposing man he was: extremely intelligent, thoroughly soaked in American as well as local history, a genealogist, a lawyer, a gentleman farmer and, for four years, our congressman in Washington. He had the deepest voice I have ever heard, and the loveliest smile and loudest laugh. Dorothy was more of a free spirit, retiring late, rising late, keeping abreast of the interests she had cultivated when Jim was a law student at Harvard. I later realized that she looked remarkably like Faye Dunaway with her finely sculpted nostrils and flowing hair. She was a Bennett, from Bennett, Iowa, and she had met Jim during the war, when both of them were captains. One of my fondest memories is of Dorothy packing Max and me into the back seat of her car, collapsing the convertible top, turning on the radio, popping open a can of beer, and driving us helter-skelter into the Iowa countryside.

I have a photograph of my own family that I keep in a silver frame in my bedroom. The four of us are tanned and relaxed, sitting at a dinner

In the Heart of the Heart of the Country

table at the hotel Harold had taken us to in Florida one winter. We're in Lauderdale-by-the-Sea and I'm probably nine at the time, celebrating my March birthday. Harold looks very contented in his white jacket and cigar. Jeanne looks as lovely and serene as ever, neither welcoming the house photographer nor shying away from his lens. Jim looks mischievous, as always, and I look . . . I look almost serene as well, I think, but with an expression that suggests that I'm wondering what will happen next. The future seems to lie all before me, although it may only have been this brief respite in a different clime, a different place, that made it seem so.

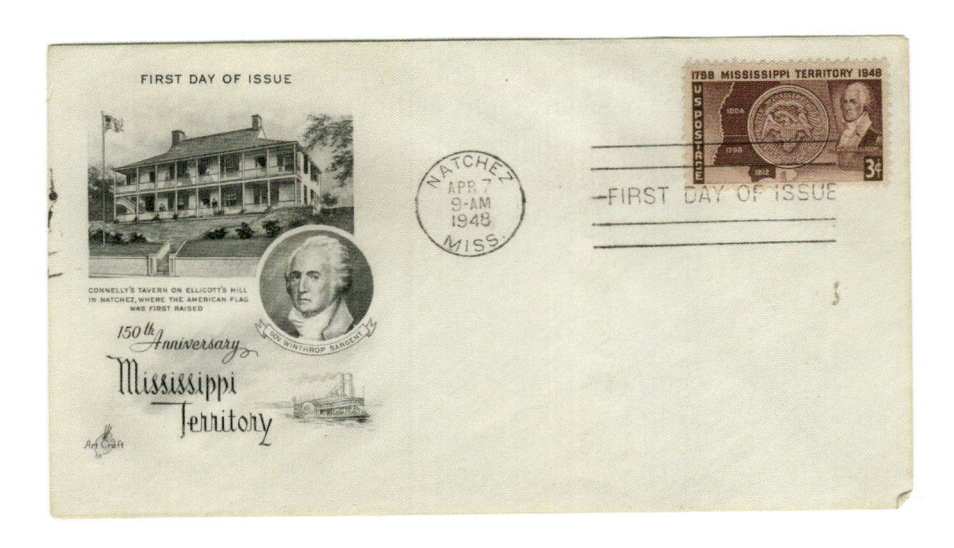

 The only pursuit I had really explored on my own at that point was as a young collector. Like many boys my age, I collected stamps and coins and made model cars out of plastic — fleets of plastic cars, as my father liked to say. But as my friends' interest in these pursuits waned over the years, mine continued to wax, especially when it came to collecting stamps. I liked the objects themselves — their various shapes and colors, the perforations, the different languages — and I suppose that some historical and geographical knowledge was rubbing off on me as well. But for the most part I valued them on aesthetic grounds and took great pleasure in arranging them in albums that I had designed and ruled by hand. When, during my middle-school years, the city held an annual contest for the best collections of any kind, I was keen to participate, putting my money down for a place to display my albums and introducing each one with a short explanation of what I found most interesting in those stamps from San Marino or the Vatican, or in albums devoted to animals, or — the center of my collection — in engraved first-day covers mapping the history of America's Civil War.

On the evening the various prizes were to be awarded, I felt like the young boy in Joyce's "Araby," trying to make sure that my family would finish dinner in time to allow me to enjoy the proceedings. But by the time I finally arrived, the lights had been dimmed and the doors were about to be closed. While my mother waited in the car, I searched the room for signs of the prizes but could find none. So I made my way to my own collection and found two objects sitting on the table: a blue ribbon for "Best Stamp Collection" and a trophy for "Best in Show."

Two decades later, when my parents made their move from the Midwest, I inherited a number of boxes containing the remnants of my childhood. When I opened the largest of the boxes and examined the collection of beautifully engraved first-day covers, I had what I suppose one would have to call a Joycean epiphany. I was surrounded, on the walls of my sitting room in Chicago, by my collection of etchings by Piranesi and other eighteenth-century *ruinistes*, and there, in the box at my feet, lay a startlingly similar collection of black-and-white images, a telling reminder that our interests may evolve over time but that they don't necessarily change.

In the Heart of the Heart of the Country

II

I WAS BORN, at mid-century, in the middle of America's heartland. But heartland, I discovered during my adolescent years, doesn't necessarily mean farmland. In the case of my own native city, the local farming community was certainly out there, all around us, but it didn't have a strong cultural impact on the way we lived. Iowa was known for corn, for soybeans, for pigs, all of which were processed at the large plants located near the center of the city: Quaker Oats (for cereal), Penick & Ford (for corn syrup), and Wilson's meatpacking company (for bacon, and for God only knows what else). One could smell the sharp odor of cereal, the sour smell of syrup if the wind headed your way, and on Friday evenings the young men at Wilson's would carry out their weekly slaughter, a pungent reminder that the city, handsome and even beautiful as parts of it were, was not a suburb of Minneapolis or Chicago.

This was still the heart of the heart of the country, even as the city struggled to define itself *against* rather than because of its rural location. I knew my cousins' farm, of course, but I didn't know the families that actually farmed it. The farm boys who attended my schools must have led pinched, demanding lives of which we could have little conception. All we saw were young men with tanned faces and white bodies, sometimes malnourished, uncircumcised, wearing odd clothes and unfortunate haircuts and using words like "ain't" and all of the "cuss" words that weren't allowed at home, let alone at school. They were the true minority students within our community: sticking to themselves, taking the rural school bus rather than a parental station wagon, often returning to the farm rather than graduating from high school.

During one of my stints as a cub reporter, I had the opportunity to attend an afternoon concert at the All-Iowa Fair by the famous country singer Eddy Arnold — and then to interview him afterwards. I was terrified by the assignment. I knew that he was an important musician; my parents vaguely knew who he was, which was somewhat reassuring; but how was I going to conduct an interview with someone whose music I had never heard? The concert was sold out. Hundreds of people, many of them dressed in their best western attire, sat in the bleachers in full sun and 100-degree heat. Much as I dreaded it, Eddy's performance turned out to be a revelation that afternoon: before he could get more than two bars into a song, the audience moved as one to its feet, clapping its hands and singing out its praise. Every song, it seemed, had sold a million records, or more: "What's He Doin' in My World?," "Make the World Go Away," and countless others. And what I realized, as I watched Eddy sing and the crowd roar its approval, was that I actually knew these songs; I knew the melodies, the pitch of his voice, even many of his lyrics. But how had I learned them? When I drove my parents' car, I would turn the knob on the radio from station to station, quickly running past the endless country-and-western channels as I searched for pop or rock 'n' roll. What struck me, that hot summer's day, was the simple fact that you couldn't entirely ignore this cultural phenomenon: it was *there*; it had somehow permeated our otherwise insulated lives.

There, for me, was a different part of the heart of the heart of the country. My native town was divided into four quadrants by the Cedar River, which runs north to south, and by First Avenue, which runs east and west. A substantial island punctuates the middle of the river, housing the city hall, the police station, and a large auditorium where I heard Gene Autry sing and saw professional wrestlers "wrestle." There was a large Czech population on the west side of the river, which was sometimes referred to as the "kolache curtain," a kolache being a Czech pastry of which my family was particularly fond. The east side was generally more prosperous, and my parents progressed through the usual scenario of trading up for larger houses until, with the departure of their two sons, they began to "downsize" themselves into smaller, more manageable ones. Long before we had area codes and zip codes, everyone living in Cedar Rapids had a postal and locational code: you were SE, NE, SW, or NW, and those dividing lines determined where you went to school and, in many ways, who your

In the Heart of the Heart of the Country

> **KINDERGARTEN PROGRESS REPORT**
>
> This report will be sent home at the middle of the year and also at the end of the school year. Parents are invited to write comments on this report.
>
> First Semester, Date __January 29, 1954__ Second Semester, Date __June 11, 1954.__
>
> ☐ has made some adjustment   ☒ has made satisfactory progress and will be promoted to First Grade
>
> ☒ has adjusted well
>
> ☐ has made insufficient progress and should be retained in Kindergarten another year
>
> Remarks:
> Richard has good work habits. He gets along well with other children and participates in all of the kindergarten activities. He follows directions *and* co-operates.
>
> Remarks: Richard shows a readiness for reading. He has a very good vocabulary and expresses himself very well. I have enjoyed having him in the group and I appreciate your co-operation.

friends turned out to be. We were "Southeast" — which my parents assured us was exactly the place we wanted to be.

The centers of my young universe were our home, my school, and the department store at which my father worked. The store was called Killian's, after the family that owned it, and my father ascended the corporate ladder just as the store itself grew in size and quality, building an annex on the lot next to it, financing a satellite store in the city's first mall, expanding to a mall in Iowa City (where the University of Iowa is located), and then, in a very strange maneuver, acquiring a boating and fishing emporium halfway between the two cities. Killian's had its own motto — "Everything for the home and family" — and it was in fact possible to buy anything you wanted there except an automobile. The main store boasted six floors, elevators, escalators, a full restaurant, a men's grill, and chocolates made on the premises (white, milk, or dark). You could purchase a mink coat, a diamond ring, a new living-room suite, carpeting, the latest books and records, radios, televisions, lawn mowers, and (my favorite department) "notions" of various kinds. The kitchen department was located next to the rifle, shotgun, and handgun display.

When we each turned thirteen, my brother and I began "taking inventory" twice a year on what always seemed like an interminable weekend. On the day each of us turned sixteen, we became regular members of the staff, selling men's accessories — shirts, trousers, ties, pajamas, socks, belts, jackets, unmentionables — every Monday evening and all day each Saturday. This apprenticeship lasted two and a half years for me, during which time I learned that the customer is always right, that madras shirts don't go with seersucker trousers, that many women (especially those from the farming community) buy their husbands' clothing, that the gay men dressing the windows were beautifully dressed themselves and having a grand time of it, and that if you passed a big sale into the hands of a senior member of the staff, someone working on commission, everyday life in the store would treat you much better — especially if you were the son of the Vice President and Treasurer, which was now my father's title.

Work, study, home life: these were the normal staples of my childhood, which was about as all-American as it could be. I learned to play baseball, football, and basketball at school and learned to swim and play golf and tennis at the country club. I was expected to excel, but not quite to stick out; to be a leader, but also to be "one of the guys." If there was ever pressure to succeed, it was softly peddled. I remember, for instance, my mother asking me about whether I would be elected to Phi Beta Kappa, the undergraduate honor society, when I was a student at Williams College. I told her that I probably would, given that there were elections at the end of my junior year and then twice during my senior year. A brief silence ensued before she said, "Oh, honey, wouldn't it be nice if you could be elected in your junior year?" And so, as a dutiful son, I managed to make it "nice" for her.

Here, in a nutshell, is how Harold and Jeanne framed their notions of what was and wasn't appropriate. When I was about to leave for college, they decided to cheer my brother up by purchasing a dog, a Lhasa Apso they called Skoshee (the Korean word for "small," which Skoshee indeed was). I wasn't sure until recently just how they came up with this uncharacteristically exotic name for their pet, but my brother had heard it used for a similar dog and that apparently made it all right. When Skoshee eventually died, my mother was heartbroken and my father decided that they should purchase another Lhasa.

In the Heart of the Heart of the Country

When they went to the farm where the Lhasas were bred, however, they fell in love with not one but two puppies, and that presented a serious dilemma for them. When my mother told me, over the telephone, that they were tempted to buy both dogs, I urged her to do so. Her reply, however, was "Oh, honey, what will our friends think?" And that put the damper on a second puppy. When I later asked her what they were going to name their new dog, she said that they weren't quite certain but that they were leaning towards "Skoshee 2." I lovingly — but *firmly* — explained to her that if their friends thought that buying two dogs was somehow an act of conspicuous emotional consumption, then naming their second pet after their first might prove to be even more remarkable — and remarkable was not within their social comfort zone. They named the dog Buffie instead.

So how, precisely, did I slowly pull away from the comforts of this pleasing, complacent, virtually strife-free environment? I argued, and I read, and I wrote my way out.

Imagine, for a moment, that you are looking at Google Earth, that you are focusing on North America, then the Midwest, then Iowa, then Cedar Rapids, and then the intersection of Third Avenue and Fifth Street. That intersection, with buildings on three corners and a small green park on the fourth featuring a small replica of the Statue of Liberty, provided me with what I needed to fashion a life that would be both similar to and quite different from the one to which I had become accustomed. On the southeast side stood the First Presbyterian Church, a handsome, impressive building of granite on the outside and stained windows and polished wood within. My parents had both been raised as Methodists. Jeanne's first cousin, Jim Bromwell, was a Quaker, and my father's cousins in Chicago had married Roman Catholics; when he was an undergraduate in college, he was strongly drawn to the Lutheran Church. My parents decided to become members of the Presbyterian congregation, however, partly because it was the establishment church community (rivaling the local Episcopalians and a step up from the Methodists and Lutherans), and partly because my aunt Maurine had become an officer of the church, serving for many years as its Secretary.

Richard Wendorf

Harold and Jeanne both taught Sunday school; Jim and I passed through "confirmation" classes and became members of the church; my father, inevitably, became a deacon.

Maurine was very close to the minister, Dr. Lilly, who liked to amuse us with tricks that he would play in his private office; he was a warm, sweet man who eventually moved to a prominent church on Long Island. His successor was not a success, and the combination of Calvin's hellfire-and-brimstone on the one hand and cold, scholarly condescension on the other made for an unhappy congregation for many years. Sunday school was even worse, with one teacher requiring memorization assignments that could not be carried out because the texts were locked up within the church. When I dared to attend church with my parents in order to peruse the various creeds, I was then berated by my teacher for not attending his Sunday school class instead. It was a no-win situation and I rebelled — against the teachers, the doctrines, and what I thought was the social hypocrisy of many of the members — and that, of course, caused difficulties at home, especially with my mother. But Maurine once again came to the rescue during one of her visits "back home," confiding that she, too, had concerns about some of the doctrinal beliefs, and urging my parents to ease off, allowing me to find my own way — which I did, on one of the other corners of Third Avenue and Fifth Street.

The Cedar Rapids Public Library had been a gift to the city from Andrew Carnegie in 1905, and I've always felt that I was one of his most fortunate beneficiaries. It's a handsome but not imposing building, still standing after the devastating flood of 1980 destroyed much of its reference and adult reading collections; it's now part of the Cedar Rapids Museum of Art. In my time, the basement was devoted to children's books and activities, the ground floor held the art, music, reference, and magazine collections, and novels and other serious books were housed in the stacks above. I spent a great deal of time there during my middle-school and high-school years: not so much reading what was available as beginning to comprehend the extent of what was available. My father was not a reader; my mother read all the time, but not serious books for the most part, and she would

In the Heart of the Heart of the Country

have been intimidated by our current rage for reading groups. What I discovered in the library was a way of navigating the various realms of knowledge, gauging how much (or how little) individual writers had published, and perusing magazines and journals that would never have a place in our own home, particularly *The New Yorker*, which I've been reading now for over fifty years.

I had been an indifferent "language arts" student for some time, keeping my head above water but not relishing the books that we were studying. The public library changed all that, convincing me that there was a larger conversation out there that might just let me in. And so I read and read, and I began to build my own collection of books, much to the dismay of a generous father whose son was racking up the largest annual bill in the Killian Company's book department. "Well, Harold," the book distributor said to him at one point, "these are fairly grown-up books your son has been ordering. Are you sure he's ready for them?" My father repeated the conversation to me, but kindly sensed that I didn't have to answer to him, only to myself.

The final step in this cultural journey took place in the third building on the intersection of Third and Fifth, directly across from the public library — the home of the *Cedar Rapids Gazette*. I'm still not sure just how my father arranged for me to have a tryout there during the summer between my first and second years of college, and of course I was genuinely worried that I would make a shambles of it, having absolutely no experience in journalism, on the one hand, and the impossibly lofty standards of *The New Yorker* on the other. But what settled me down was the sheer professionalism of the staff: if I could edit a bit, write a bit, make my deadlines, then they were happy to accommodate me. I learned to write quickly and directly, to compose on a typewriter, to proof as quickly as I had written, and to make those deadlines at noon and two-thirty. The *Gazette* had a style sheet that still keeps me honest today. Odd jobs led to a few feature articles, a few book reviews, and finally my own byline, at first well hidden within the pages of a fairly substantial evening paper, and then — much to the amazement of my parents — right there on the front page (although below the crease). I was nineteen years old, then twenty, then twenty-one during what turned out to be three invigorating summers, and I would never again have so many readers during my entire professional career.

When my parents decided to move to Scottsdale, Arizona in 1982, I cannot say that I was disappointed. A winter's vacation in the desert, mountains, and sun of the American Southwest was a godsend, as my mother would have said. And there were galleries and antiques shops and desert gardens to explore, as well as an entirely different vision of American history. But my parents remained good Midwesterners. They joined the local Presbyterian church, my father raised money for burn victims through the Shriners' temple in Phoenix, and the same food came to the table every time I visited them over a twenty-five-year period. They made new friends, mostly among people who had also moved down there from Iowa, Illinois, and Minnesota. They

In the Heart of the Heart of the Country

enjoyed their new surroundings. They embraced the warmer climate and never missed the snow that was falling each winter on the city they had left behind. But they always maintained that the Midwest was a good place to come from — and that's a conviction I continue to maintain, immatour as that belief may turn out to be.

CHAPTER TWO

Teaching Is What It Was All About

If you grew up on the west side of Cedar Rapids, you attended Jefferson High School; if, like me, you lived on the east side, you went to Washington. Most of the schools in my hometown were named after presidents. My elementary school, named after the ubiquitous Grant Wood, was an exception. When my parents moved us across some invisible border in the southeast quadrant of the city, I was transferred to Johnson Elementary School (Andrew, not Lyndon), and thence to McKinley Junior High School, where my aunt Maurine and her friend Grant Wood had taught when it was still a high school in the 1930s.

George Washington Senior High School was one of those bland, modern, attenuated complexes boasting only two stories, cracked cement tennis courts, and barely enough parking for all of the cool kids driving their parents' Mustangs and Pontiac GTOs. I was not cool. I was interested in sports but was not an outstanding athlete, barely scraping together a junior-varsity letter on those blistered tennis courts. I was thought to be from a wealthy family because of the department store in which my father worked; that didn't help either. And I was bright, bespectacled, and very serious about my coursework (the social kiss of death). I made some good friends, I learned what it was like to be an outsider in a culture quite different from what I had hoped it would be, and I performed as best I could, not graduating first in that class of 748 students, but third, trailing two friends who went on to have distinguished careers in chemistry and biochemistry. I was not a happy camper.

But there were compensations, of sorts. The first was the sheer size of the student body — three classes of over 700 students each, packed into a building that had been designed for a much smaller cohort of hormone-driven adolescents — and that situation allowed for a certain

Teaching Is What It Was All About

amount of anonymity as well as for various courses taught in Quonset huts built in front of the school. The second benefit was a required course in public speaking during one's first year. I was, of course, petrified by the prospect of standing in front of even a small class of students and making a proper speech, but the course was taught by a kindly woman who made it as painless as possible. My final presentation was a speech, with drawings, chronicling the history of beards in England. I have no idea why I chose this very strange topic, but I do remember how I managed to begin it without panicking that I would forget my lines. I simply counted to three in my head (one, two, three) and then commenced my talk with the next number: "For some unknown psychological reason, the male beard tends to reach its fullest flower when a queen sits on the throne of England."

She liked it (which was good) and she insisted that I enter various speech contests in the Midwest, representing our school (which was not good). But I reluctantly agreed and adapted the talk for a much larger audience (hundreds, in one case) and for the television cameras. Much later, when my parents were about to move to Arizona, my father asked what they ought to do with the trophies. I told him to take them to the high school and convince the principal that they should be included with all of the sporting trophies. My father returned home, trophies in hand, and I suppose they eventually made their way to the local rubbish pit.

There was another consolation as well, for Midwestern high schools in the mid-1960s attracted some exceptionally talented teachers. I was the beneficiary of four of them: Señor (Doctor!) Paul Díaz, who taught us the intricacies of Basque fiction; Larry Olsen, who taught an honors course that combined American history and literature; and Dick Hubacek, who pioneered a similar course on European literature and history. Larry was a warm and engaging teacher who more or less adopted several of us for the year. Dick could be haughty at times: he had very high standards and wanted us to take American and European culture as seriously as he did. He was thin, taut, and supremely in command of the classroom. This, I thought, was what college would be like, and his course was augmented by a three-week whirlwind tour of Europe: London, Oxford, Germany and Switzerland, Venice, Florence, Rome, and Paris. We were required to learn elementary expressions for each country, how to negotiate the different currencies, how to use the subway in London and Paris and the local buses in Rome. Before seeing what turned out to be my first opera — *Aida*, in the Baths of Caracalla — we listened to a lecture as well as to the complete score. This, I thought, was what life *after* college would be like.

And then there was Donald T. Hollenbeck. To most of the students in the honors English courses he taught, he was an old-fashioned, unreconstructed martinet, quite capable of reducing students to tears either directly, in class, or when they read his withering responses to their written work. I naturally adored him, and I probably owe many of my own intellectual aspirations to the example he set. The year spent with him was an immersion in close reading, in irony, in grammar, in sentence and paragraph structure (yes, we diagrammed our sentences, a now unheard-of form of pedagogical torture), and we wrote and wrote and wrote, sometimes extremely short essays, sometimes not. It was survival of the fittest. Mr. Hollenbeck even smiled — occasionally. Among all of the school reports and essays that my parents religiously retained years after I had graduated, there was one exercise from Donald's course that I was particularly proud of, a character sketch of the concierge at the Hotel Valadier in Rome.

Teaching Is What It Was All About

And of all those reports and essays that my parents eventually passed on to me, it seems to be the only one that is missing. I occasionally wish that I could see to what extent my work as an eighteen-year-old may have prefigured the kinds of writing I have published since then. (But then again, I might well be quite embarrassed by such an encounter with my adolescent self.)

During the summer before my final year in school, my parents and my brother and I ventured forth to make the obligatory tour of various colleges. My parents would not allow me to consider a university: too large, they said, and too far away. And so we visited a handful of Midwestern liberal arts colleges, all of them fine academically but all of them situated in small towns surrounded by cornfields. I tried to convince them that we should look further afield, so to speak. They consulted with my "guidance counselor" about how best to place me. He informed them that there was no point in visiting colleges on the East Coast; our Midwestern colleges were just as good. But then a small miracle occurred. Some of my classmates began to make the tour of Eastern colleges and universities — and Stanford as well — and their parents asked my parents which colleges in the East they wanted *me* to apply to. Harold and Jeanne hemmed, they hawed, and they finally folded. We packed up the car again and toured Williams, Amherst, and Trinity. I didn't take much to Hartford, so Trinity was out. I loved the catalogue of courses at Amherst, the college's focus on basic academic requirements across the curriculum, and its roster of teachers in the English department. But then we visited Williamstown, situated in a valley surrounded by hills and mountains rather than cornfields, with two museums, a repertory theater company, and an undergraduate guide who drove up in a green-and-white Austin Healy 3000. Williams had also recently abolished its fraternity system, which very much appealed to someone who often felt out of place in his socially stratified high school.

And so Williams it was — and not just for me, but for two of my classmates as well, much to the amazement of those students in the class of 1970 who came from areas that had quotas imposed upon them, such as Westchester County. "Where's Westchester?" I asked someone in my dormitory whose family lived in Rye. You can imagine the look of disbelief that came my way. There were other major adjustments to make as well. Although my fellow students were extremely bright and accomplished, they tried very hard not to show it. This was a new code of conduct that I didn't do very well in following, I'm afraid. Many of them seemed to know each other already, or to know people in common, or to be part of extended families that summered together in Maine or the Adirondacks or Martha's Vineyard. Some of the upperclassmen had purchased vintage fire engines and held parties on them before home football games, driving and drinking with some abandon down the streets of little Williamstown. Some of them would talk about their stock portfolios as I hitched a ride to the college's ski slopes. And they were all men! After thirteen years in fully coeducational schools, I found myself completely bereft of female friends, let alone potential lovers. I didn't know a single woman who attended one of the Seven Sisters, and when I went to mixers or was set up with a blind date, I fared very badly indeed. By the end of my first year, I thought very hard about transferring to a coeducational institution and had received invitations from Stanford and Michigan, Jeanne and Harold having finally relented on the ban they had imposed on universities. But there were, as always, real compensations in that purple valley, and Williams has remained a part of my life over the past fifty years as I have returned there both to consult and to teach.

 I attended my first class at 9 o'clock on a Tuesday morning; it was the introductory philosophy course, taught by Sami Najm in a cold, bright room off the back of Stetson Library. There were few preliminary statements. Najm simply lit his pipe, flashed his mischievous smile, and said, "Well, Mr. Wendorf, what *is* philosophy?" I was panic-stricken and speechless; I finally told him that I wasn't sure. The course met three times a week — including Saturday mornings — and Sami Najm asked me the first question at the beginning of the class *every* time we met throughout the fall semester. In the spring he finally, mercifully, began calling on other students, but I was never entirely let off the 9-o'clock hook.

 Few of my classmates will remember Sami Najm, who never became a senior member of the faculty at Williams. He was a Lebanese whose immigration status, I was told, forced him to take a position in Canada at the end of the year. But he knew what he was doing, and he did it well; and his principal task, I finally saw, was to make us realize that philosophy, beginning (as we did) with Plato's *Republic*, was a lengthy conversation — a dialogue of engagement — and that our own responses and tentative gropings were no less important than his difficult acts of interrogation. Perhaps the most revered exemplar of this interrogatory mode was Robert Gaudino, whose introductory political science course I took during my second year. Gaudino was also a smiler — and he also gave very little away. I remember more than one occasion when, at the end of seventy minutes of intense questioning, he sadly shook his head, told us that he was sorry that we "gentlemen" had not yet understood the issue at hand, and quietly left the classroom.

Experiences such as these could be quite devastating, and I think that all of us shared similar episodes in which someone made us feel uncomfortable, accountable, part of a larger intellectual community. We didn't have mentors, we had *provocateurs*, and many of them were legends in their own time. Take James Clay Hunt, for example, a Southern blue-blood from Lexington, Kentucky who was so wound up in his subject (Milton, in my case) that he couldn't wait until the bell rang before beginning what was a dizzying, digressive, fluorescent monologue that even the final bell could not quite muffle. David Stern '65 put it this way: "Once he arrived, a characteristic tic signaled that Mr. Hunt was ready to begin. His (left?) hand touched his chest, his head pulled back, thrusting out his chin, as if he were harnessing himself to his teaching load or adjusting his flak jacket for close combat." He was notorious for opening his first class of the semester by saying, "Ma name is Clay Hunt. Clay rhymes with lay and Hunt rhymes with cunt, an' I don't want any fuckin' around in this course!"

Clay taught himself Italian and gave a similar course on Dante. He knew his classical music and he knew his contemporary ballet, once proclaiming to our class that "living in America today and not experiencing Balanchine's choreography is like living in Renaissance Rome and refusing to see what Michelangelo was up to." He had published a well-respected book on Donne and seemed to know most of Yeats by heart. At the close of my first essay, on "Lycidas" (a poem I still approach with fear and trembling), he said that I wrote beautifully but that the essay itself was "a crock of shit." He accused me of being a "prep-school dilettante." I went to see him during his office hours, assured this Southern aristocrat that I had not had the benefit of a boarding-school education, and asked him for advice for my next essay, on Dryden's *Antony and Cleopatra*. He liked that essay — "Well, this is a mighty different litter of pups!" he wrote at the top of the first page — but I found the entire semester to be harrowing, not the brightest moment in my as-of-yet not-so-brilliant undergraduate career.

Much more to my taste was the intimate cut and thrust of those smaller seminars led by equally gifted teachers. Larry Graver was a delight in the classroom: quick of wit, engaging, willing to entertain opinions of all kinds while maintaining his own high standards (which I didn't quite meet). I studied the twentieth-century novel with him and gratefully drew upon that experience when I found myself in the same role at Northwestern many years later.

Teaching Is What It Was All About

Larry had a wry, bemused take on the craziness of the world at large and took his solace, I think, in the richness and complexity of the literature devoted to that world.

Larry's close friend Peter Berek, who taught me Chaucer, Spenser, and Shakespeare, was equally intense in the classroom, and I remember telling him years later that we were reluctant to answer his questions because they were so ingenious that there could never be such a thing as a straightforward answer to them. In the mid-term examination, for instance, we were asked to apply E. M. Forster's distinction between "flat" and "round" characters in fiction to Renaissance texts. I thought that I had managed fairly well, only to be told that a truly incisive essay would have questioned the validity of Forster's distinction as well as its applicability to the literature of an earlier period. Peter remains a good friend — and one of the most incisive critics of my writing to this day.

The core series of courses in English literature stretched over three years, from *Gawain* to *Ulysses*, but the historical chronology on which these courses were predicated was almost entirely devoted to *literary* history, with almost no linkage to the social, political, or cultural issues we explored in our other courses. We wrote essays on the battle of Culloden during our first-year European history course, for instance, but the larger eighteenth-century context in which Pope and Johnson and Fielding wrote was intentionally neglected within the English major. I cannot remember being asked to read a modern critical essay or book devoted to any of the writers we read, let alone a biography. It was intensive, old-fashioned close reading, the "new criticism" erected upon a chronological backbone. For the relationship between literary texts and the history and broader artistic culture of the eighteenth century, I would have to wait until Williams generously sent me on to Oxford.

But there was an exception, a loophole in the otherwise tight fabric of the department of English, and that was the proximity of the Chapin Library, located within a wing of the handsome building in which we met for most of our classes and in which our teachers had their offices. Many years later, when I became the Librarian of the Houghton Library at Harvard, I learned that the founding director of that institution had chosen to attend Williams rather than Harvard or Yale as an undergraduate because the Director of the Huntington Library, near where he grew up in southern California, had told him that he would never be able to work with the rare books at those universities, whereas the Chapin Library had been established precisely for that purpose. And so many of my fellow students and I were unwittingly following in the footsteps of the legendary William Alexander Jackson, he whose work on the English Short-Title Catalogue earned him honorary doctorates from both Oxford and Harvard.

Teaching Is What It Was All About

Jackson was a "book man" to his very bones, and so were the "custodians" (yes, we only recently retired that title) of the rare book and manuscript library at Williams. In occasional seminars held in Chapin during my final three years, Richard Archer would produce the books in which our texts originated, together with important examples of how some of those texts had been illustrated and embellished by later figures, particularly in William Morris's work on Chaucer and Mallory at the Kelmscott Press. We didn't engage in original research in the Chapin Library, but we understood that it held another form of literary history, focused on material objects, on their making and re-making, on the relationship between text and image, and on the history of printing as a rich subject in its own right.

Thinking back on my four years in the Berkshires, I realize that we idolized our teachers in that hard-nosed, irreverent style that Williams so quickly instilled in us. One of my friends proposed, during a public meeting on the possibility of the college becoming coeducational, that we fell in love with our teachers because there were no women on campus to whom we could direct our affections. Well, we certainly made wild excuses for them when they strayed too far from the accustomed path. Some of my friends were taught Freshman English by the legendary Don Gifford, a brilliant if somewhat idiosyncratic figure who had taken a double first at Cambridge and who was compiling a comprehensive companion to James Joyce's novels without the benefit of the Internet and without ever setting foot in the Republic of Ireland. When Gifford didn't promptly return his students' essays in that course, and still hadn't returned them after the second essay was due, my friends began talking in hushed tones about the severe problems he was experiencing with his eyesight. Years later, when I returned to Williams to teach in the department for a semester, I told Giff this story over dinner one evening and he shook with laughter. His eyesight had, of course, remained perfectly fine.

Again and again we were the recipients of an unusual and precious gift, for we were taken seriously by a faculty that insisted on putting us on the spot and by an administration that granted us extraordinary latitude in governing ourselves. Harvard undergraduates,

Richard Wendorf

as I later learned, often find it difficult to get to know the famous professors who lecture to them — and whom they read about in *The New York Times* — but they retreat from their classes to an elaborate housing system filled with graduate students, deans, resident faculty members, senior common rooms, and a benevolent master. Like many other liberal arts colleges, Williams has defined its own sense of community and responsibility in a completely different way, lavishing attention on its students in the classroom but refusing to serve as the arbiter of undergraduate social and cultural life. The college has changed in many ways in recent decades: it has a coeducational faculty and student body, it has grown in size, it is a much more diverse institution, and it is also immensely rich, with an endowment well over $2 billion. These are all significant improvements, but I sense that the central focus on teaching — on the encounter between individual students and their teachers — has not changed an iota. James Garfield, the only president the college has produced so far, famously said that his idea of a perfect education was to place a student on one

Teaching Is What It Was All About

end of a log and the college's charismatic teacher and president, Mark Hopkins, on the other. The student body has changed; the faculty has changed; but the encounter between them remains the same.

At a reunion dinner several years ago, I heard some classmates at the other end of the table virtually howl at each other as they told stories about "Charlie Samuels." I couldn't hear exactly what they were saying; it was enough to know whom they were talking about and to hear the timbre of their voices as they did so. No one, of course, actually called Charles Thomas Samuels "Charlie." That was their disrespectful way of leveling the playing field, and there was a great deal of leveling to be done, for Charles Samuels was just as brilliant as he was intimidating. He was not unlike many of the gifted, prickly scholars I have gotten to know at Oxford, Princeton, Northwestern, and Harvard. But Charles Samuels was different: he taught for a living.

Although he was primarily an Americanist, offering seminars on Faulkner and James, Samuels also introduced the study of film to the college, and I was one of a handful of students who spent the winter-study period in January 1969 watching and talking about films with him in the basement of Weston Hall. The sessions stretched on and on, and some of the students eventually brought their pillows with them. The course was enticingly called "Antonioni or Hitchcock?" — a juxtaposition that introduced us not only to the work of those two filmmakers but also to questions of genre, cinematic grammar, the interplay of camera and dialogue, the role of the actors, and the divide (if one existed) between high art and popular entertainment. It was a heady experience; at least two of us went on to teach film ourselves; and it was critically compelling. Charles Samuels could be a confrontational, divisive figure. He entitled one of his books *Encountering Directors*; his course was not entitled "Antonioni and Hitchcock" but the more oppositional "Antonioni *or* Hitchcock." We were constantly forced to defend our positions.

Somehow Charles and I hit it off even though his sole comment on my essay on *Blow-Up* was "Good," and during the snowy months that followed he used to call me in my room in West College and ask if I wanted to watch a film that he had been able to rent. He hoped, at first, that I would run the projector for him, but he continued to invite me to join him even after I had demonstrated my mechanical ineptitude. We once watched *Le Jour Se Lève* at midnight, leaving the Bronfman Science Center in the middle of an achingly cold and beautiful night. There was no log, and God knows that Charles Samuels would have been appalled by any comparison with the respectable Mark Hopkins. But those evenings defined, at least for me, precisely what was special about the place. When I think of my years as an undergraduate there, I inevitably begin with Sami Najm and end with Charles Samuels, his disturbingly intense face focused on the flickering screen until, as the credits began to roll, he would turn to me and ask, "What do *you* think?"

CHAPTER THREE

(Yet Another) Yank At Oxford

SHORTLY AFTER the Boston Athenæum re-opened its brass-studded, red leather doors in 2002, I was asked, as its director and as an Oxonian, if I would host the annual Oxford and Cambridge Society's Christmas dinner. I was something of a veteran of these affairs, both in Chicago and later in Boston, and I usually looked forward to them with a mixture of anticipation and dread: anticipation because I enjoyed seeing old friends and making new ones, dread because of the empty toasts and sometimes mind-numbing speeches. In Chicago, the more exuberant participants would declare the night still young after the final benediction and go out dancing (and even more drinking), which explains why I twice discovered a long-lost credit card in the pocket of my dinner jacket an entire year later. In Boston, on the other hand, everyone would bid each other a polite goodnight and head straight home to bed after a mildly soporific evening. But once, just once, I was able to listen to an after-dinner speech in Boston that was both clever and quite funny, and I had therefore been wondering for some time whether I, too, might be able to carry off such a nuanced performance. And so I screwed up my courage and told the Society's secretary that I would indeed host the annual dinner — and that I would present the after-dinner remarks as well.

My decision was based partly on the opportunity I would have to show off the Boston Athenæum following a renovation and expansion program that took three years and over $30 million to complete. But I was also moved by the ways in which that earlier speaker, Ved Mehta, had been able to hold his audience in the palm of his hand by re-creating his experience as an *ingénue* at Oxford: Indian by birth, blinded by illness when he was four, schooled in the United States, and then magically transported to England. Mehta's years at Balliol were presented as a succession of surprises and misunderstandings about which his younger self could only ask, "Would you believe

Richard Wendorf

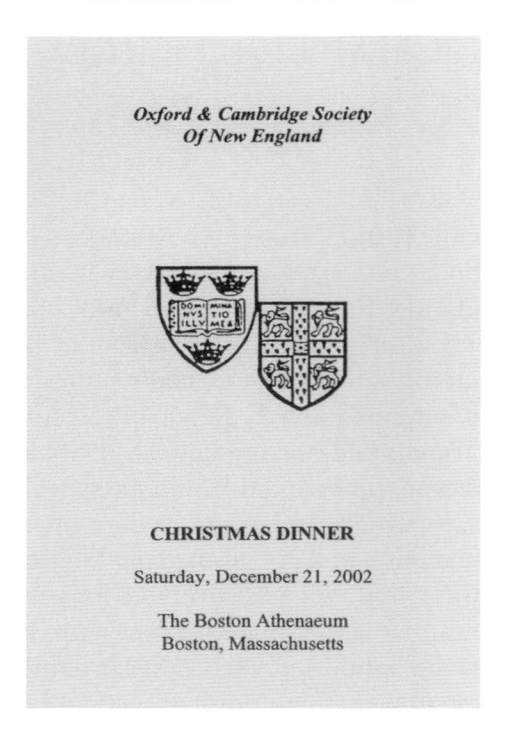

> **Oxford & Cambridge Society
> Of New England**
>
> **CHRISTMAS DINNER**
>
> Saturday, December 21, 2002
>
> The Boston Athenaeum
> Boston, Massachusetts

this?" and "Would you believe that?" How, precisely, could I, so different from Mehta in every possible way, approximate the blend of humor, nostalgia, and acute judgment that had made his remarks so... remarkable? I was worried, to say the least, but I had decided to take a chance.

And now a short digression. I had known and admired Ved Mehta's writing for many years, introduced to his memoirs of life in India with his mother (*Mamaji*) and father (*Daddyji*) in the pages of the *New Yorker* before moving on to his own early autobiography in *Face to Face*. And just a few years earlier, while sitting in my office at Harvard's Houghton Library, I had received a phone call from my secretary asking whether I would be willing to speak to "a Ved Mehta, who is on the line." Indeed I would — and did — and this led to an exchange of books and lunches that meant a great deal to me. To anyone seri-

(Yet Another) Yank At Oxford

ously interested in the sound and texture of English prose, Mehta was (and still is) a modern master.

I had therefore set my sights rather high, and I had further elevated my anxiety index by inviting my wife, Elizabeth, my brother, Jim (Christ's College, Cambridge), Jim's wife, Jessie, and various Bostonian worthies, including some of my trustees. But I knew that I had two important factors certain to work on my behalf: in the first place, the subtle beauty of the rehabilitated Athenæum, which would absolutely glow on a cold December evening; and in the second, and perhaps even more important place, the sheer amount of decent wine that my audience would be drinking before, during, and after our dinner. I wasn't the main course, I reminded them; I was the dessert; and by the time I got up to speak, they were in a very jolly and pliant mood indeed.

I began by describing how perplexing Oxford could be, with its rules and regulations and traditions, many of which were never written down and some of which we were paradoxically expected to violate. I had rather odd introductory conversations with the college physician ("You don't really need to take that medication, do you?") and with Worcester College's quite formidable provost, Lord Franks, who asked me to evaluate the importance of Samuel "Hudibras" Butler, whose works had been meticulously edited by my principal tutor, John Wilders. Like Ved Mehta before me, I quickly wondered what exactly these people were up to, because it was clear that Franks didn't think much of *Hudibras*. At the end of my two years, the college physician made an even more problematical remark (which I cannot repeat here, much as I would like to), and the provost, noting that he was about to receive an honorary doctorate at Princeton shortly after I was to arrive there for my doctoral work, smiled and said that he would be pleased to say hello to me if we were to meet on the pavement there.

When remarks such as these came my way, I often wondered if they were prompted by the simple fact that I was an American: that I was somehow being addressed as a generic figure — too friendly, too innocent, too over-medicated — rather than as the person I knew myself to be (or at least aspired to be). And, in all fairness, American students in the early 1970s did tend to congregate together, perhaps all the more so because of limited living accommodations, marriages, and a tendency to have a little more disposable income in our pockets and bank accounts than many of our British counterparts. We were often given the impression that we were different, even supernumerary (to invoke one of those wonderfully creaky Oxonian terms). And, in 1970, our time at Oxford was played out against the background of the conflict in Vietnam, which did not endear us to many of our contemporaries no matter what our own personal beliefs might have been. But Oxford had long been, as Matthew Arnold put it, the "home of lost causes, and forsaken beliefs, and unpopular names, and impossible loyalties." We were part of a much more heterogeneous culture than I was used to, and many of us realized that we needed to try harder, needed to downplay our relative affluence, needed to become part of the social fabric of the place.

Fortunately for me, my academic and "moral" tutor at Worcester College, John Wilders, very much liked America and Americans, had studied and taught at Princeton, and would eventually split his academic year between Oxford and Middlebury College in Vermont. John was a breath of fresh air at Worcester, writing plays for the radio, insisting that we drink sherry with him as we read our tutorial papers, and then coaxing me out the back door of his rooms so that we could play a few games of squash on the college grounds: before

(Yet Another) Yank At Oxford

noon, of course, and therefore breaching one of the college's unwritten rules. When I purchased a pair of gray bellbottoms and a red bowtie, both in velvet, from Herbie Frogg on Jermyn Street in London, he quietly confessed that he wished he were young enough to wear them himself. And he certainly would have. John was not theatrical in person but very much a denizen of the theatre; years later he would write introductions to Shakespeare's plays when the BBC commissioned productions of all thirty-seven of them. They remain, to my mind, models of their kind.

But John was not my only tutor. I studied early seventeenth-century English literature with him and with a recent Harvard graduate, Fred Fisher, once a week, both Fred and I producing short essays on either drama or poetry. But we also had to study medieval English literature as part of the undergraduate curriculum, and we therefore met every two weeks in a small seminar with the college's other English tutor, Meg Twycross. Mrs. Twycross was youngish, energetic, and eccentric — a combination that I would discover in several members of the English faculty. Unlike John, she enjoyed but a single room and had devised an unusual filing system in her cramped quarters: instead of placing essays and assignments in a filing cabinet, she tucked them away in a large series of Viyella shirt boxes, presumably inherited (or borrowed) from Mr. Twycross. She was well-known throughout the university — or at least among the young men at the university — for wearing short skirts and paying scant attention to what they might reveal. When we met for the first time, she described the outline of our work together that Michaelmas term, distributed various pieces of paper from various Viyella boxes, and then turned to me and said, "Mr. Wendorf, would you please prepare an essay for the seminar on the *lais* of Marie de France for our next meeting? Thank you very much."

Only at the college for a week, I thought to myself, and already singled out for conspicuous duty. But I purchased the English translation of the *lais* of Marie de France at Blackwell's, read through them until I could say something remotely intelligent, and then wrote an essay that I presented to the group in two weeks' time. I cannot, in all honesty, remember whether my remarks prompted any discussion among my counterparts or whether Mrs. Twycross decided to use the essay as a point of departure for her own contribution to the seminar. But you may well wish to forgive me my failing memory because, at the end of our session, she turned to me once again and said, "For our next meeting, Mr. Wendorf, I wonder if you would present an essay on the *lais* of Marie de France. Thank you very much." And with that she stood up and proceeded to place her notes in one of those blasted shirt boxes.

There was dead silence in the room. I looked down; everyone else, I'm told, looked at each other in utter amazement. Once we were out the door, Fred Fisher asked me what in the world I was going to do. "Only one thing to do," I told him. "I need to have a talk with John Wilders."

I was, of course, handing John a tricky dilemma because, although Mrs. Twycross was his junior colleague and a university lecturer rather than a fellow of the college, there were (it occurred to me) certain shadowy conventions that probably obtained in such cases. Worcester didn't have anyone else who could teach me medieval literature, and it was not advisable, he explained, for me to be sent to another college for tuition, as it was called. So, he concluded, either I remained in the undergraduate program and continued with Mrs. Twycross or I could apply, with his reluctant support, to enter into a graduate program, incongruously entitled a bachelor of philosophy degree: two years of tutorials with specialists in a specific field followed by examinations. John was willing but not entirely happy to nominate me for such a

(Yet Another) Yank At Oxford

program, he said, because he thought that I had a good shot at obtaining a "first" in my current program. I would also, he pointed out, be starting the graduate degree a term late, thus ruling out the option of writing a mini-thesis during my second year. I hemmed, I hawed, I consulted my friends, I talked with students already in the graduate program, and I finally decided to see if I could make the leap. And that decision, I hoped, would lead me to an extraordinary cohort of scholars, all specialists in Restoration and eighteenth-century literature, which was the historical period I had chosen.

I had to undergo an interview first, of course. The director of studies was the Reverend Graham Midgley, fellow and dean and chaplain and vice-principal of St. Edmund Hall. I adored him at first sight: a tall, gangly, mostly bald Yorkshireman with incredibly long fingers, dressed in comfortable corduroys and with a mischievous look in his eye. His rooms were a wonder to behold. Leather everywhere: on the spines of most of his books, on the patches on his sleeves, on various satchels and briefcases and gun bags. He didn't offer sherry, only a martini that he referred to (as certain people did in those days) as a "gin and French." The antique furniture and running bookcases were punctuated by modern pieces of sculpture, which I later learned were the work of those long fingers of his. Years later he asked if I'd like to take a look at his bedroom: white walls, an old-fashioned servant's bed, a crucifix hanging above it, and a shotgun propped in the corner.

As preparation for my interview, I had been told by a friend that Midgley had recently delivered a talk on "cats in literature" at the local women's institute. True, he answered, "but I don't really like them, cats that is. Fred! Come here, old boy!" Seated as I was, in a very low leather chair, the yellow Labrador that made his entrance into the room looked as large as the proverbial hound of the Baskervilles. And he was enormously friendly, almost frighteningly so. "You do like dogs, don't you, Richard? Because Fred is part of the company here." As he said this, he took a postcard off his desk and presented it to me: it was a photograph, sold by the college, of the Reverend Graham Midgley and Fred appearing as modern gargoyles on top of a recently restored Anglo-Saxon tower at Teddy Hall. When

Fred died several years later, Graham wrote a short epitaph for his gravestone:

> Beneath this turf the Dean's dog Fred
> Without his master, goes to Earth, stone dead.
> But on the tower, stone Dean and Fred together
> Enjoy the sunshine and endure bad weather.

"Nice likeness, don't you think?" he asked me. "Especially of Fred."

That was question number two. The third was more academic. Students in the program had to choose a special author for one of their examination papers. Only four were listed: John Dryden, Jonathan Swift, Samuel Richardson, and Samuel Johnson. I knew Dryden's work fairly well — and would soon study it again with Graham and John Wilders. Ditto with Swift. Richardson was an unknown quantity: I only knew *Pamela*, and only the first of those two volumes, and my heart sank as I thought about how many volumes were devoted to *Clarissa* and *Gran-*

dison. "Don't blame you," Graham said; "entirely too sentimental." Had I been able to choose Pope I would have done so; but Johnson was the other important figure during this period, and I welcomed the variety and vitality of his work. So there it was: I liked dogs, I liked Fred, and I liked Johnson. I had answered all three questions correctly and had been accepted into Graham's orbit, filled with muscular authors, muscular dogs, muscular sculpture, and muscular Christianity.

And what an orbit it turned out to be! In addition to working with Graham and John, I had the chance to study the eighteenth-century novel at Balliol with Roger Lonsdale, with whom I had earlier studied at Trinity College, Oxford, during the summer between my third and fourth years at Williams. Roger had agreed to write on my behalf as I applied to enter Oxford on a full-time basis, remarking to me that he would not be writing an "American-style" recommendation suggesting that I was the next T. S. Eliot. Whatever he wrote, it seemed to have worked, and he and I have remained scholarly colleagues ever since. I was also "farmed out," as people were in my program, to other colleges throughout the university: to David Fleeman at Pembroke, the bibliographer of Johnson, whom I wished I had been able to work with on a much more protracted basis, and to Michael Gearin-Tosh at St. Catherine's, whose baroque lectures on satire I could make absolutely no sense of. He and Mrs. Twycross, I later realized, served as similarly eccentric bookends to my experience at Oxford. But firmly placed in the heart of that experience was the time I spent with two remarkable figures, both of whom would have a lasting influence on my development as a scholar.

The first was David Foxon, whose last name was already a point of reference in the scholarly world. David was Reader in Bibliography at Oxford, a position that, as it turned out, had ill-defined duties and a decent sprinkling of academic prestige. "Foxon" referred to the two fat volumes listing every individually published English poem between 1700 and 1750: a massive undertaking that Roger Lonsdale would later replicate by reading all of those poems as he prepared his editions of eighteenth-century poetry (and poetry written by women) for Oxford University Press. Graham knew that David was working on an ambitious new project, and he persuaded him to offer a seminar for one term, in the bowels of the New Bodleian Library, to which all six B.Phil. students would be invited. Some of my colleagues were skeptical, but I was intrigued, still harboring warm memories of my experiences in the Chapin Library at Williams.

Foxon struck me, during the first session we spent with him, as more of a scientist — a forensic specialist — than as a literary scholar. He was interested in pinpointing certain changes within the publication of Pope's poetical works and in demonstrating how carefully Pope prepared his manuscripts for publication, even to the point of designing introductions to his "moral" or "ethic epistles" that looked as if they had already been printed. By focusing on Pope's authorial methods, on his relationships with his printers, and on the various editions his poems passed through, Foxon concluded the session by suggesting that the editorial decisions of the scholars who had recently published the multi-volume Twickenham edition of Pope were essentially flawed. And with that pronouncement he called the seminar to a halt and said that he would see us again the following week.

But when a week had passed, there was no Reader in Bibliography in sight. Foxon had shown us quite different ways of thinking about the dissemination of literature, and he had drawn our attention to the importance of balancing manuscripts against the printed editions they would (largely) become. But, having engaged and tantalized us, he simply disappeared. We made inquiries, of course, but were never really given a proper answer. Several years later, as I was working on an edition of William Collins's poetry that would become my dissertation and first book, I tracked Foxon down, living on a small farm outside of Oxford. I had been told that he had relinquished his work as a bibliographer because of failing eyesight, and yet he rather proudly showed me the furniture he had been creating and restoring in his barn. He had, it turned out, been able to deliver his thinking about Pope and the eighteenth-century book trade as a series of Lyell Lectures at the university, and one of his students, James McLaverty, later saw them into print. It is, I believe, one of the most interesting books published in my field, and his focus on the capitalization of common nouns during this period represents a strong precursor of my own work on the development of the modern book in English.

I must admit that I felt shortchanged by David Foxon's sudden disappearance, but by that point, well into the second year of my studies, I had learned to take most Oxonian surprises in stride. What remained for me, in my final term, was an opportunity to work with Graham's closest colleague in the program, Rachel Trickett, who was a senior fellow at St. Hugh's. I had chosen "biography and autobiography" as one of my set subjects, and because Miss Trickett rarely had a student willing to undertake this rather eclectic set of texts, I was allowed to study with her. I dutifully made my way to north Oxford, wondering what it would be like to work with someone who was already a living legend among her students and peers. Not perhaps as famous or formidable as Dame Helen Gardner, who ruled the English faculty and terrorized the staff of the Bodleian Library, but legendary in her own right.

As I attempt to reconstruct my experiences at Oxford, I am particularly aware of the succession of rooms in which I made my precarious way. First John Wilders's comfortable set at Worcester, with its back door leading to the inviting squash courts beyond. Mrs. Twycross's much more cramped space, with its menacing shirt boxes. Graham Midgley's masculine set, complete with gun and dog and martini shaker. Roger Lonsdale's large room at Balliol, with eighteenth-century prints and a complete run of the *Gentleman's Magazine*. The strange space in which we encountered David Foxon that one and only time: perhaps, in retrospect, a conservation laboratory in the lower depths of the New Bodleian. And then, finally, Rachel Trickett's library, an elegant room suffused with light and featuring bookcases that reached from floor to ceiling. To my left, as I sat there with her for our first meeting, was a wide expanse of window looking down on one of the college's quadrangles. Miss Trickett also took a seat, although she had a habit of rising every so often to find the right book or piece of paper. She was in her late forties when I met her and had already published an important book on eighteenth-century poetry and several novels, including *The Course of Love*. I found her to be a lively and yet comforting figure with a soft face and thinning auburn hair. But if she looked rather Miss Jane Marple-ish, that illusion quickly evaporated as she laid down the guidelines for our term together and began to dictate what I would read.

    By the time I was released, I realized that a list of what I *wouldn't* be reading that spring would be much shorter than the one I had in hand. Pepys and Evelyn, Johnson and Goldsmith, Boswell and Frances Burney — most of them in multi-volume editions that would make the attendants at the Bodleian groan for eight full weeks. And I also, of course, wanted to read the scholarship devoted to Boswell and Burney in particular, because we had agreed that I would write my essays on the two late eighteenth-century figures who were the beneficiaries of so much earlier biographical and autobiographical writing. I therefore spent three weeks immersed in Boswell's *Life of*

(Yet Another) Yank At Oxford

Johnson and its variegated predecessors before dropping off a rather long essay at St. Hugh's in preparation for our next meeting. That encounter went rather well, I thought. Miss Trickett seemed not to be displeased with the shape of my argument (I choose the double negative deliberately, of course) and sent me spinning into the arms of the young Frances Burney and her playful diaries. I was in heaven, excited by what I was reading and now feeling, for the first time in my academic career, that I was genuinely on top of my subject. I found a nineteenth-century edition of the diaries at one of Oxford's many antiquarian bookshops, wrote an even longer essay on Burney, and waited with anticipation for our final meeting.

That interview, however, went about as well as the young Jack Worthing's encounter with Lady Bracknell in Algernon's handsome set of rooms in Albany. It wasn't that Miss Trickett disagreed with what I had written; it was simply, she explained, that I was barking up the wrong Oxonian tree. "Richard, Richard," she began, "you have written long essays that are fine in their own right, but they will not enable you to pass your examinations and receive your degree. You need to be synthetic in your approach. You need to tell your examiners that you understand the development of biographical writing in this period, with all of its twists and turns. It's fine if you want to turn these essays into your doctoral dissertation, but you won't leave Oxford with a degree unless you know how to write a proper examination paper."

And then, as she rose and began to consult various books on her shelves, I was privy to one of those performances that had made her the object of so much interest. As she turned from one text to another, she knew precisely where to open the book and find the appropriate passage. As excerpt followed excerpt, so did the outline of biographical writing during this period. Finally, as she searched for a book without success, she looked out that broad expanse of window and told me that she would have to dictate from memory — and this she did, for a considerable period of time. And this, I realized, was part of the mystique that enveloped her, based on an extraordinary power of memory that we might conveniently describe as photographic. But it wasn't photographic, as I later learned — or at least it wasn't entirely a case of remembering what she saw on the printed page. Her father, a postman in Wigan, had recited Shakespeare and Gibbon, Macaulay and Tennyson to her when she was a child, and she had been able to build upon that experience in her life as a writer and teacher. At the close of our meeting I felt chastised, I felt empowered, and I felt that I had been in the presence, if all too briefly, of a remarkable person.

The title of the talk I delivered to my well-lubricated guests at Christmastime in 2002 was "Down Thirty Years and Still Sorting It Out," and I suppose that I am still engaged in that interpretive process today. By focusing on the gifted and sometimes eccentric teachers who had given me tuition during my two years at Oxford, I was deliberately leaving out many other aspects of university life that we have also carried away with us, both for better and occasionally for worse. And thus in my closing remarks I also paid tribute to the friends we had collectively made during our careers there, the academic rituals we had passed through and, perhaps most important, the opportunities we had, as young Americans, to begin to see the world through rather different cultural and political lenses — some of them provided, free of charge, by the National Health Service. Re-entry into American life after two formative years abroad was not as smooth as I had thought it would be, even within the comfortable confines of the graduate school at Princeton. My experience in England had altered me in various ways, and it had also created a social and intellectual reservoir which I have been able to draw upon throughout the decades that have followed.

And my audience that snowy evening in Boston? Well, they clearly liked the episode about my brief encounter with medieval English literature at Oxford — especially those blasted filing boxes — and they cheered when I concluded my talk by holding up my copy of the *lais* of Marie de France and declaring that I had never (nor *would* ever) purchase a Viyella shirt. But afterwards, as the tables began to be cleared and most of our guests headed towards the door, a handful of the society's members came up to me and quietly confided that it

(Yet Another) Yank At Oxford

was entirely too easy to forget about those extraordinary people who taught us decades ago. By focusing on those auspicious moments, I was clearly touching a nerve of some kind. Warm (or at least interesting) memories seem to have been rekindled, and I took comfort in the thought that, at least for a few minutes, we had added our intellectual encounters to those perpetually cheery remembrances of commem balls, college gaudies, and the annual boat race.

CHAPTER FOUR
As Ever, Charles

O NE OF my friends at Williams, Barry Bartrum, had graduated a year before me, had read English at Cambridge for two years, and had more recently begun his doctoral work at Princeton in Victorian literature. He was handsome, short, social, chatty, effeminate, and wonderfully bright; comparisons to Truman Capote were more often made than not. Barry was the first person I saw when I arrived on campus, and we became lifelong friends, keeping that friendship alive in Chicago after we both took our degrees. Barry immediately told me that although the English department boasted of a very low student-to-faculty ratio, quite a few of those faculty members were "hiding under rocks" and that he hadn't yet laid eyes on them. I had made the decision to attend Princeton partly because it was a small program with generous scholarships, and partly because Lawrence Lipking taught there and I wanted to work with the author of *The Ordering of the Arts in Eighteenth-Century England*, which I had "wolfed down" (as my mother would have said) during my second year at Oxford. And I did work with Larry, both as his graduate student and then, a few years later, as his colleague after we lured both him and his wife, Joanna, to Northwestern. What I didn't realize when I made my decision, however, was that the director of graduate studies, Henry Knight Miller, was a distinguished Fielding scholar, and that Earl Miner had just been hired away from UCLA to teach the English Restoration as well as Japanese literature at Princeton. These were unexpected riches indeed in the "long" eighteenth century, and there were junior faculty members soon hired in the same period as well as the promise of a special collections library with strong holdings in early books and manuscripts.

I kept hearing, moreover, about yet another scholar in the field, always with affection and even reverence: "Oh, you must meet Charles at some point. He's often here on the weekends." I hadn't read the poetry of William Cowper when I was studying at Oxford and therefore hadn't come across Charles Ryskamp's critical biography of the poet's early years, nor had I twigged to the fact that the editors of one of Boswell's later journals were "Ryskamp and Pottle," a scholarly partnership begun when Charles was a graduate student at Yale. But Charles Ryskamp wasn't hiding under a rock: he was commuting to Manhattan every Monday morning to run the Pierpont Morgan Library while simultaneously editing Cowper's poems and letters with two of his former graduate students, John Baird and James King. He was a very busy person indeed, and the question hanging in the humid New Jersey air in the autumn of 1972 was whether he would have time to offer another graduate seminar at Princeton. Charles did have the time — and that decision changed my life in ways that I could not possibly have foreseen.

It turned out to be Charles's final graduate seminar at Princeton, and it was an immersion in serious scholarship and professionalism that not all of my classmates immediately relished. There were only five or six of us, a small cohort but rather larger than the graduate seminar Frederick Pottle once offered at Yale that enrolled only two students, Charles and Harold Bloom, an unlikely pair if ever there was one. We met every other Monday, and on most of those Monday mornings we were expected to turn in assignments that were completely new to us: cataloguing visual motifs in Blake; editing a Cowper letter from the original manuscript and with complete annotation; writing a letter of inquiry to the aristocratic owner of a private collection ("Whatever you do," he told us, "don't actually send them!"). And then, as the seminar came to an end, he invited us to join him at the Morgan after it closed for the day so that he could share some of the treasures in the library's vault with us.

Several months later Charles invited me to meet him at his home on Cleveland Lane in Princeton. I think that I was penciled in between a lunch with one local grandee and dinner with another, but Charles could not have been more welcoming, showing me his collection of books and drawings, sharing his belief that rooms should have multiple functions, and giving me a glimpse of his garden — designed by Bunny Mellon — behind what, to most passersby, must have looked like a rather modest house. We sat down to tea and he came to the point. In addition to having contracts with Oxford University Press for editions of Cowper's poetry and letters, he also had a contract for an edition of the works of William Collins, to be published as an Oxford English Text, the pinnacle (at least in those days) of scholarly editions. Would I consider preparing this edition as my dissertation?

    I was completely surprised, and although I was naturally grateful for such a generous and complimentary invitation, I also found myself in a rather difficult dilemma. I wasn't sure, in the first place, whether I really wanted to spend two years preparing a scholarly edition, and I also found Collins's poetry to be very, very difficult: heavily allusive, often rather stilted, and often rather idiosyncratic. I was, by this time, fairly well steeped in the poetry of Dryden and Pope, Johnson and Smart, Gray, Cowper, and Blake, but Collins had always remained the odd bloke out. And then there was the dissertation that I *thought* I was going to write: a study of biographical writing in the eighteenth century, supervised by Larry Lipking and returning me once again to the world of Burney and Boswell. What to do?

    I consulted my friends in the program, who wondered why I would even think twice about not accepting such an offer. And I talked with Larry, who immediately counseled me to accept it as well. Working with Charles and preparing an edition would be an interesting experience, he said. He would happily serve as the second reader, and I could always return to Johnson and Goldsmith, Boswell and Burney for my second book, reminding me that I would actually have an Oxford book in hand very early in my career. For the next two years I therefore sat in Charles's "Cowper and Collins" office in the bowels of Firestone Library, gazing at a print after Canaletto of the rotunda at Ranelagh Gardens above his desk, and taking a short nap whenever my eyes fogged over from comparing different copies of the same

As Ever, Charles

edition in a Hinman Collator, located just a few yards away in the offices of the Thoreau Edition. I did a lot of typing — endless typing, it seemed at times — a form of torture that would eventually change with the advent of personal computing. (Indeed, the entire conception of a scholarly edition would soon change with the introduction of multiple and layered texts made possible by electronic technology.) But in those days, in the mid-1970s, we still did it the old-fashioned way, with a manual typewriter and many jars of White-Out.

Once or twice a month, on a Friday, I would deposit an installment of the edition in the oversized gray mailbox outside Charles's front door; on Sunday afternoon I would meet with him to discuss my progress and the various problems that had arisen. Was Collins well enough — was he sane enough? — to have made stylistic changes in later editions of his work? What should we make of changes introduced in Robert Dodsley's anthologies? How should we deal with the fact that the first edition of the *Persian Eclogues* was printed with heavy italics and capitalization whereas the second edition was almost completely modern in its appearance? How heavily should we annotate this most allusive of poets — and how should we acknowledge the many annotated editions that had already appeared, stretching from the early nineteenth century to Roger Lonsdale's recent (and copious) volume? I raised the problems; Charles weighed them, talked them through with me, and very generously (and I hope correctly) agreed with my solutions. When my work was complete, handed over to a professional typist, proofread, defended, and bound, Charles invited me to lunch at Lahiere's — the small, elegant restaurant on Witherspoon Street cherished by Princeton's more affluent residents — and presented me with an early edition of Collins's work. The edition itself was not that special, but Charles bent the text block within the leather covers and displayed a beautiful fore-edge binding, a pastoral scene inspired by Collins's "Ode to Evening." Inside he had written, "for Richard Harold Wendorf from his fellow student of the eighteenth century, his friend, and occasionally his teacher, Charles Ryskamp. 30 July 1976."

Richard Wendorf

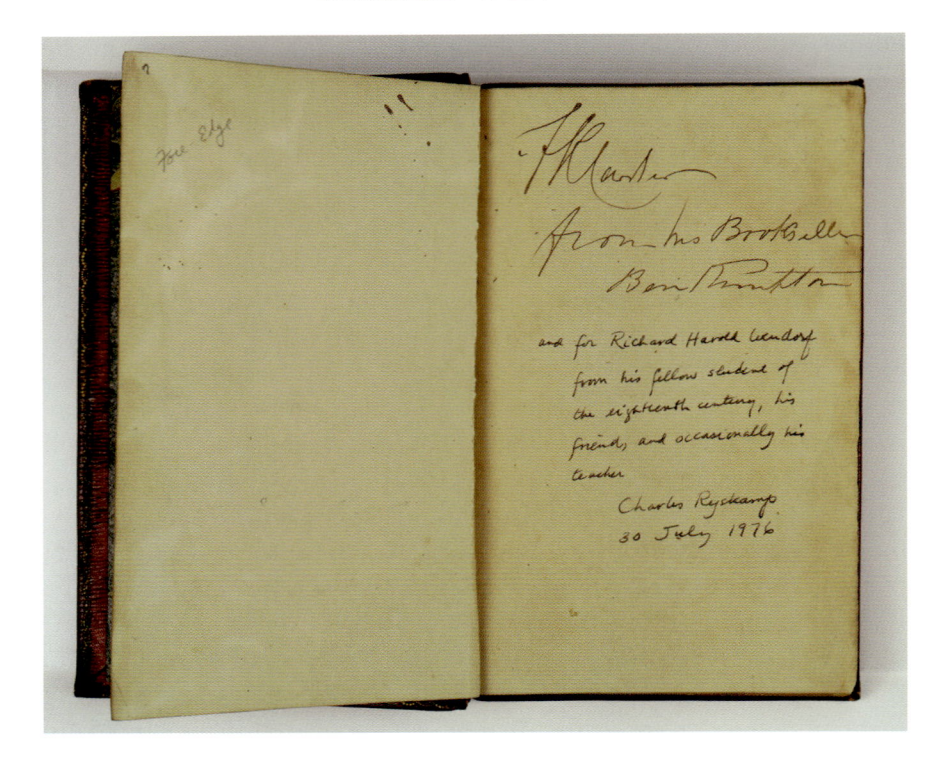

By academic standards (perhaps by any standards) Charles led quite a glamorous life. He squired Jackie Kennedy around New York and an aristocratic woman sporting a black eye-patch around London. He stayed with the Devonshires at Chatsworth and with the Mellons on Cape Cod. He belonged to the right clubs — Century, Grolier, Roxburgh, Turf — and served as a trustee of the Guggenheim and Mellon foundations in New York and of the Amon Carter Museum in Texas. He was written up in *Town and Country* and in *House & Garden*. He was knighted by the Queen of the Netherlands, stayed (and played Scrabble) with her in the royal palace, and became godfather to one of her grandchildren. He was photographed by Beaton as well as by the ubiquitous Ron Galella. His friends lavished drawings, prints, and books on him, all of which (he told them) would eventually make their way to the Frick Collection or to the Morgan Library.

As Ever, Charles

When I told Charles that Barbara (my wife at the time) and I were hoping to find a caretaker's cottage on an estate near Princeton while I was preparing my edition, he said (as only he could), "Well, I only know of one cottage available at the moment, but I'd be happy to look into it." A few days later I was introduced to Grace Lambert, whose Pink House was located just on the outskirts of the town. Grace had inherited the estate from her husband, Gerard Lambert, an immensely successful businessman who had helped to give the world Listerine (from what would eventually be called Warner Lambert Pharmaceuticals) and, later in his career, Gillette blue blades. Jerry had made his mark in the business world when advertising and marketing were in their infancy — and he did so before the imposition of a federal income tax. Grace therefore enjoyed several hundred acres of orchards, farm land, and woods, with a swimming pool situated above a haw haw, a stable filled with Morgan horses and donkeys, and a kennel packed with yellow Labradors. One of the yellow retrievers, Missy, had the honor of serving as a "house dog"; a very large black retriever named Nemo also enjoyed that privilege. And I enjoyed the privilege of living in Grace's gardener's cottage for those two years of textual editing: walking the dogs, harvesting the apples, and growing basil and tomatoes in an old-fashioned cold frame off the back of the cottage.

My obligations on the estate were few and far between. I was supposed to harness the snow plow to a Jeep when necessary and plow the long drive that led from the road up to her house, but that was beyond my competency and one of the workers took charge on the few occasions when it actually snowed. I handed out enormous chocolate bars in the front hallway of the Pink House on Halloween, which was tantamount to holding off a stampede of young trick-or-treaters all hellbent on placing one of Grace's oversized gifts in their goody bags. When the pack of retrievers drove the cats up into the trees, I learned how to bring them down with the aid of a water hose. And on various weekends my wife and I were enlisted to join Grace and her guests for Sunday lunch, complete with a Danish butler (Teddy), finger bowls, and some of the finest claret I have ever tasted (and which Grace herself could not drink). Teddy taught me how to make the perfect Bloody Mary, which he had concocted on Jerry Lambert's boat when he used to race against King George V. You must keep it simple, he said: just combine tomato juice, vodka, lemon juice, and Worcestershire sauce, shake it with ice, and then strain it into glasses. Teddy had no use for hot sauce, celery, or celery salt, let alone the green olives that have recently made their appearance — and neither do I.

Just before our second Christmas on the estate, a case of wine arrived at our door from the Wine and Game Shop in Princeton. I thanked Grace for such a generous gift, but I was privately disappointed because the box contained twelve bottles of white wine — six French, six German — rather than the claret I had begun to enjoy at her Sunday lunches. I placed the box in the basement of the cottage and thought no more about it until we gave a dinner party several months later. I refrigerated the French bottles, all bearing the name Puligny-Montrachet, which I had never heard of. That dinner produced a revelation, of course, for our guests had also never tasted anything quite so lovely, and I basked in the aura of that dinner for several weeks. I eventually decided that I should buy some myself, so I drove to the wine shop on Nassau Street, introduced myself to the chap behind the counter by reminding him of the case of wine Mrs. Lambert had purchased for us, and told him that I wished to buy some myself. He smiled and told me that he couldn't sell that particular wine to me. "Why not?" I asked. "Because you can't afford it," he replied.

When I was well into my work on the edition of Collins, Charles also introduced me to Mary Hyde at Four Oaks Farm, just a short drive north from Princeton. Mary and her late husband Donald had assembled the greatest private collection of works by and about Samuel Johnson (as well as other figures, including the Elizabethans and Oscar Wilde). Mary invited me to Sunday lunch, for which I thought I was prepared, given my experience at Grace Lambert's table — but I was in for an uncomfortable surprise, because there were quite a few guests gathered together for pre-prandials in her library, including Walter Jackson Bate. I was absolutely terrified, and all the more so when Mary pulled a first edition of Johnson's *Lives of the Poets* from a shelf and asked me to read Johnson's life of Collins to the entire group. That turned out to be fairly smooth sailing, but making small talk with Jack Bate, the greatest Johnsonian scholar of the century — and a great Keatsian and Coleridgeian as well — was hard work until I mentioned that I had read his most recent book, *The Burden of the Past*, and could just about place Collins within the argument Bate had so eloquently made there. Much later in my career, when I arrived at Harvard's Houghton Library, Jack and I became good friends, he orchestrating membership in two clubs he enjoyed (Boston's Saturday Club and Harvard's Cambridge Scientific Club), I interesting him in sorting through some of the materials relating to Keats in our collection. And thus what had become one introduction by Charles led to many others, given the warm scholarly environment that bound so many extraordinary people together.

Richard Wendorf

By introducing me to Grace Lambert and to Mary Hyde, Charles had given me a glimpse of the public, social side of his life that so many people knew. He had already presided over the emergence of the Morgan Library as a dazzling, star-studded institution and would later move uptown to the Frick, where he had his own private chef and dining room and, once again, breathed new life into one of the country's patrician institutions. He once showed me his diary while he was still at the Morgan: each evening of the week, Monday through Thursday, he had written in three engagements. Because he felt that he couldn't turn down his various patrons, he would accept an invitation for drinks in one apartment, dinner in another, and dessert and after-dinner drinks in a third. He lived, for many years, in a dinner jacket, and like the Duke of Windsor he believed that midnight blue looked even darker and richer than black in artificial light. The pace of his public life would have been strenuous for a much younger person, which made his weekends in Princeton all the more precious.

What was not that evident to the cultural world in which he flourished was the fact that Charles rigorously maintained his life as a scholar. He once told me that some of his hostesses refused to believe that he actually wrote books and articles: "Oh, Charles," one told him, "that's impossible!" He would rise early and read proof on the Cowper and Collins editions before walking across 39th Street to the Morgan each morning. When he stayed with the Mellons and the Devonshires, it was with the understanding that he would be able to work in the afternoons. Once a year he would fly to the Caribbean, check himself into a hotel, read on the beach, and turn to his scholarly work. Although he had little time to read through my installments after I dropped them off at his house on a Friday, he was always prepared for our meeting on Sunday afternoon.

I don't think that Charles ever set out to be a mentor, but he certainly set a powerful example for the younger scholars whom he attracted. By watching him in action, I learned how to dress properly for New York and London, how to interact with colleagues and donors, and how to write a proper thank-you note on a properly engraved card (he always ended his, "As ever, Charles"). These are not entirely superficial characteristics, for they taught many of us how best to represent the institutions placed within our care. But what I admired most deeply was how generous and gracious he was — and what I saw was how those qualities created a warm filigree of attachments and associations with those around him. When our edition of Collins was ready to go to the press, he said that there were two ways of presenting our names on the title-page, either as "Wendorf and Ryskamp" or as "Wendorf with Ryskamp," insisting that my name go first. I chose the former, of course, intending, in a small way, to repay his own generosity.

It shouldn't be forgotten, moreover, that Charles began and concluded his remarkable career not as a library or museum director but as a teacher, rising through the ranks of the English department at

Richard Wendorf

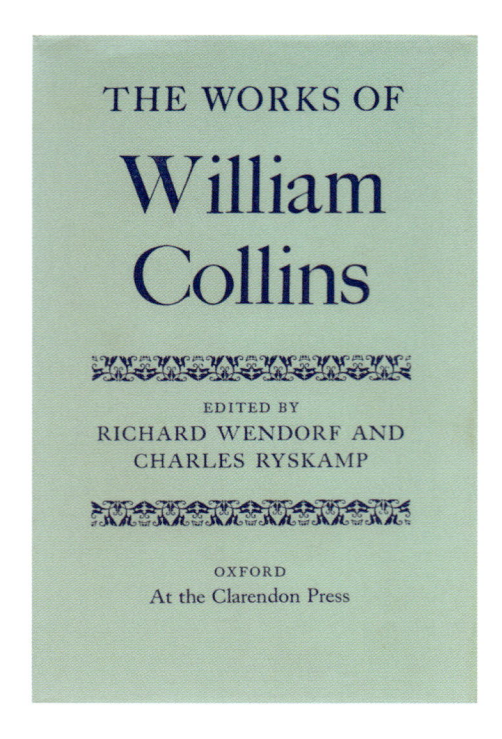

Princeton and then, in the final years of his life, working with undergraduates in New Haven as he prepared his exhibition of European Romantic drawings at the Yale Center for British Art. He was just as at home in the classroom as he was in a library or an English country house. Or perhaps I should more accurately say that any environment in which he found himself *became* a virtual classroom as Charles did what Charles did better than anyone else of his generation: convincing his students, his colleagues, his benefactors that what they were discussing was of the greatest importance — and often of the highest quality. Whether Charles was talking about William Blake, the conductor James Levine, an unknown artist in Brooklyn, or the best Italian coffee on the Upper East Side, he spoke with such authority and conviction that those around him were usually transfixed. He once told me that he never actually asked people for money; he simply

As Ever, Charles

told them what the Morgan or the Frick needed to acquire, exhibit, or safeguard — and the rest is history.

My fondest memory of Charles in the last decade of his life is of meeting him for lunch in New York and then being led (yes, at the age of 50 and then some) from one m useum or commercial gallery to another as he admired (surely not for the first time) what was on view. On one such visit, I was entranced by a small watercolor portrait of Warren Hastings by George Stubbs, which — while verging on the miniature — had great power and sympathy, capturing the face of someone who had endured a seven-year impeachment trial in the Houses of Parliament at the hands of Sheridan and Burke. Charles noticed my interest and agreed that it was very fine but, unfortunately, very expensive. When I attended the opening of the exhibition at the Morgan Library devoted to his collection of drawings a year later, I wasn't entirely surprised to see that Warren Hastings had a place of honor on one of the library's walls. Charles had claimed the lovely Stubbs for his own before passing him on to all of us, courtesy of the Frick Collection. I have always felt

Richard Wendorf

privileged to be personally in his debt, but there were so many in the cultural world who were touched, in one way or another, by his ardor and by his remarkable eye.

CHAPTER FIVE

An Inconvenient Revelation

Preparing a scholarly edition is demanding and often tedious work, and during my final semester at Princeton I was eager to find some kind of academic alternative, an escape valve, something that might stimulate and entertain me at the same time. I decided to audit John Rupert Martin's upper-class course on Baroque art, which met twice a week in a small lecture theater perched above the university's art gallery. Martin was a gentlemanly scholar of the old school, properly attired, mustache atwitter, and almost unbelievably eloquent as he led us from Caravaggio and Borromini through Rubens, Bernini, and Velázquez. One of his assistants confided to me that when he read one of Martin's lectures to the class during the professor's absence, he discovered that Martin had accentuated each important word or phrase, marked out appropriate pauses, and even included a few "ahems." It was, in other words, an entirely scripted performance, one that earned him (if I remember correctly) the only perfect teaching score at Princeton (5 out of 5) year after year.

Martin was a remarkably versatile teacher, well practiced in producing the traditional juxtaposition of images *à la* Wölfflin (Bernini on the left, Borromini on the right) but also adept at mixing genres and media — painting, sculpture, and architecture — to great effect. He was also committed to the probing and extensive interrogation of individual works of art, which was still something of a novelty in the world of art history at that time. And much to my satisfaction, he extended the scope of his course into the Rococo, concluding with a session devoted to Hogarth. I was somewhat familiar with Hogarth's prints from my course at Oxford, but they were introduced in what was essentially an illustrative gesture — another way of viewing the social history of the period. Martin's approach was quite different. He spent time examining the pictorial structure and the undulating brushwork of Hogarth's paintings before turning to the print version

Richard Wendorf

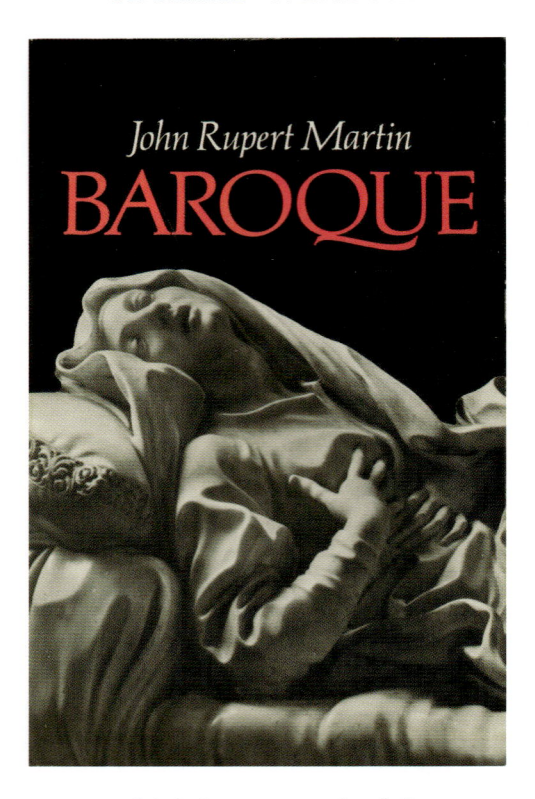

of *The Rake's Progress*, which he approached first as a narrative, then as a collage of iconographical motifs to be decoded, and finally as a repository of written signs and texts that needed to be interpreted as well. After the challenging work of the late Michelangelo and the mannerists, after the glorious color and pageantry of Rubens and Velázquez, after the refinement and power of Bernini's Rome, one might have found the middle-class moralizing of William Hogarth to be something of a letdown. But that wasn't how Martin saw it. And for someone like me, steeped in the literature of the period, he provided a way of thinking about the visual art of the seventeenth and eighteenth centuries that opened up entirely new intellectual and aesthetic possibilities.

This was an exciting moment in my life — and it was also a deeply perplexing one. I had spent the past ten years studying English literature (for the most part), six of those years at the graduate level. I was about to move to Chicago to begin my teaching career in a high-powered English department at Northwestern. And yet, as I sat in my seat in the back row of that auditorium on the final day of John Rupert Martin's course, I realized that what I really wanted to do — or, at the very least, what I *also* wanted to do — was to teach and write about the visual arts. It was, as Al Gore might say, an inconvenient revelation.

I had, of course, some basic training in art history. Like almost every student at Williams in the 1960s and 1970s, I had taken the introductory courses taught by Whitney Stoddard, Bill Pierson, and E. J. Johnson, who (together with Lane Faison) were responsible for turning out what has long been called the "Williams Mafia" in the museum world, securing directorships or presidencies at the National Gallery, MOMA, LACMA, RISD, the Getty, the Guggenheim, and the Art Institute of Chicago. But I was not of that ilk, and even in my coursework outside the English major I had turned my attention to the ancient world, studying Greek history, Greek tragedy, and two years of classical Greek. The Clark Art Institute in Williamstown was a beacon and a solace, and the proximity of Princeton to New York made many other museums almost as accessible. I had written a long essay in Charles Ryskamp's graduate seminar on visual and verbal motifs in Blake, and Charles himself was a perfect example of someone who had been able to combine literary and visual art in his scholarly as well as in his professional life. But as I left Princeton for Chicago, I still felt like the young Keats with his nose pressed against the shop window.

I was fortunate that Northwestern came quickly to my rescue. The department of English turned out to be an unusually accommodating environment in which to work. Even young assistant professors were offered the chance to design their own courses, the teaching load was quite manageable, the students were more often than not highly intelligent, and there were senior members of the faculty who shared many of my own interests. At the center of my new universe stood Jean Howard Hagstrum, author of a book on Blake and of the seminal text in the study of interartistic relations, *The Sister Arts*, which I had read as a graduate

Richard Wendorf

student at Princeton. Leonard Barkan (in the Renaissance) and Carl Smith (in American studies) were equally welcoming, and once we persuaded Larry Lipking to join our cohort, we had a formidable line-up indeed. I was allowed to teach a course on film in my second year, and then to devise an interdisciplinary course on the Enlightenment with my colleague in the French department, Bernadette Fort. Bernadette introduced me to Watteau, Boucher, Fragonard, and the *salons* of Denis Diderot. I introduced her to Hogarth, Reynolds, and Gainsborough, which enabled me, in lectures and seminars, to build up my confidence in approaching the visual arts. By the time Leonard Barkan and I became full professors, we were welcomed into the department of art history as well, happily sporting two titles and not so happily attending twice as many departmental meetings.

The story I've just sketched sounds serendipitous indeed, and I was obviously the recipient of an unusual degree of freedom in what I did and how I did it, watched over by the indulgent eyes of department chairs and by a remarkable philosopher-dean. (For a taste of just how energetic that dean remains in retirement, you might visit his blog, characteristically entitled "Rudolph H. Weingartner: Home of Strong Opinions.") But that's the external, the institutional narrative, and it actually stretched over thirteen years, years in which I struggled much of the time to find an appropriate way to approach those "sister arts" in the eighteenth century. There were not many examples from which I could benefit. Most of the scholarship devoted to eighteenth-century British art was still in the dominant mode of connoisseurship, chronological history, and *catalogues raisonnés* — all of which were tools to be utilized but none of which offered the practical criticism so prevalent in the study of English literature and only tantalizingly glimpsed in Martin's course on the Baroque. The seminal work of Michael Fried, T. J. Clark, Linda Nochlin, Griselda Pollock, and Michael Baxandall was still to come. Robert Wark at the Huntington was encouraging, but he rightfully warned me that art historians didn't welcome interlopers and that I would have to master the basics before I aspired to anything else. The sole example of what *might* be accomplished came not from an art historian, moreover, but from Ronald Paulson, and I probably owe more to the example of *Emblem and Expression* than to any other single work.

I had other obligations to attend to at the same time. Having seen the edition of William Collins's poetry into print, I was finally ready, I thought, to write about the poems themselves, which I did in a monograph that positioned his work within the broader matrix of eighteenth-century poetry. I was asked to work part-time in the office of the undergraduate dean, which I actually found quite interesting, and I continued to nurture my ambition to write about biographical narrative in the eighteenth century. But how best to do this? Another chronological survey? A juxtaposition of Johnson and Boswell? A comparison of diaries and journals with more formal and public biographical writing? The answer — or at least *my* answer — came to me while I was supposed to be working on Collins during a research fellowship at the Huntington. The resources of the library were marvelous, but what I found even more stimulating was the collection of Henry Huntingdon's paintings, housed in what was originally his own home. They were mostly portraits and mostly from my period, and just as I had taken a weekly walk to the Clark when I was an undergraduate, so now I took a daily stroll to the gallery, where I looked, and thought, and began to take notes.

To what degree, I asked myself, are the formal and informal portraits hanging on those damask-covered walls examples of biographical encapturement — or even narrative? How might one compare, or at least juxtapose, a verbal portrait with a visual one? How often were engraved portraits included in the original publication of those biographies? And if they were included, did they become part of the way in which a biographer unfolded his or her story? By the time I left San Marino, I had at least the outline of what a comparative study might look like, perhaps a chapter in my book on biographical writing. But then that rather vaguely imagined chapter began to take over the entire enterprise. Might it be possible to extend my scope back into the early seventeenth century, examining the work of Izaak Walton, on the one hand, and Van Dyck on the other? Could one compare the brief lives of John Aubrey with the contemporary art of the miniature? Were there "double agents" who practiced both arts? To what extent did the triumphal forms of biography in the seventeenth century survive in the more secular texts of the eighteenth? To what extent did the iconographical motifs of Baroque portraiture survive in the seemingly more naturalistic portraits of the following century? There were many intriguing figures and problems to tackle, and the result was my longest and (at least so far) my most ambitious book, *The Elements of Life.* But while the conception of this book came fairly quickly, it enjoyed an exceedingly long gestation, complicated by an invitation to become the undergraduate dean and by my continuing search to find the right way, chapter by chapter, to frame my analysis and juxtapositions. And, in the long run, it enjoyed the fate of many interdisciplinary ventures, with literary scholars praising the sections on painting and art historians praising the sections on biographical narrative. *C'est la vie. Ou du moins la vie académique.*

One of the aspects of scholarly work I've therefore found most intriguing is the way in which one aspect of a proposed study can actually expand to such an extent that it becomes not just the entire book but a significantly larger project as well. This seems to have become a pattern in most of my writing, although at the time I have never actually seen it as such. Once my work on *The Elements of Life* was completed, for example, I decided that I would attempt to write an entire book on one artist, diving into the art historical waters wholeheartedly. But once again there were choices to be made. Van Dyck, Reynolds, and Gainsborough were all lacking a major critical study; only Hogarth — thanks again to Ron Paulson — had received this kind of interpretive attention. I found myself particularly interested in Reynolds, not least because his life and work intersected so closely with other figures in whom I took a similar interest: Johnson, Boswell, Burney, Goldsmith, Sheridan, and Burke. I constructed the outline for such a study and then began reading through the biographies devoted to Reynolds and the journals and miscellanea in which he made an appearance. What I discovered was a consensus among Reynolds's friends and patrons about the painter's ability to *please*: he emerged as an exemplar of what was called complaisance and complacency in the eighteenth century. As a consequence, the material that I thought would form the core of an introductory chapter once again took over the entire book — and not just this book, published as *Sir Joshua Reynolds: The Painter in Society*, but its successor as well.

Because the material I had discovered was so extensive, I had been forced to make a decision about whether to include the evidence I had collected about Reynolds's death and burial in the monograph or to publish it separately, either as individual essays or as part of a collection. The monograph on Reynolds was long enough (and, I thought, it held together well enough) to publish as it was, without the two additional chapters. And thus with the encouragement of Brian Allen at the Paul Mellon Centre in London, I wrote those two additional essays and then launched into similar enquiries about the nature of evidence in art history, focusing on questions of attribution (in Raeburn), of signification (in Stubbs), and the interplay of painting, text, and frame in Rossetti. The published volume, *After*

Richard Wendorf

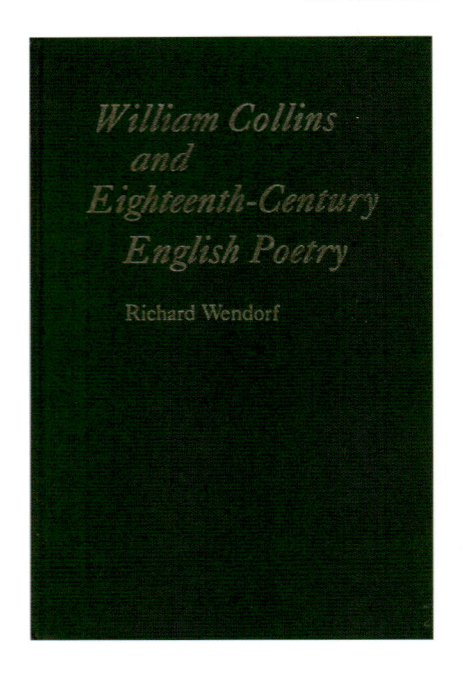

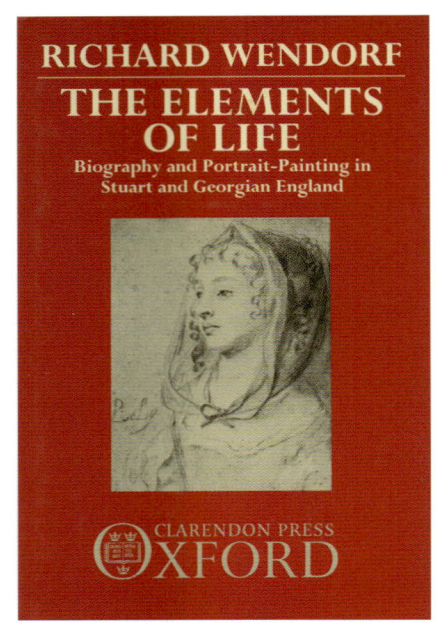

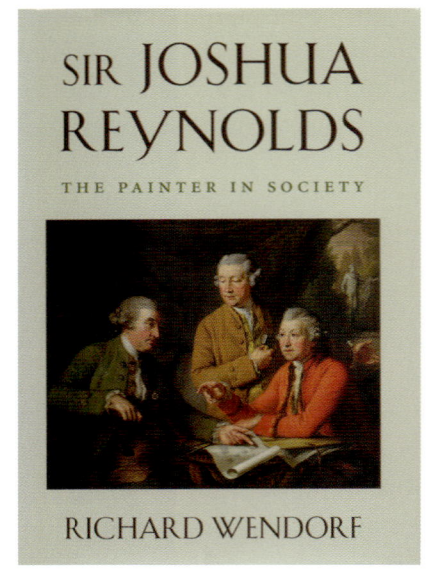

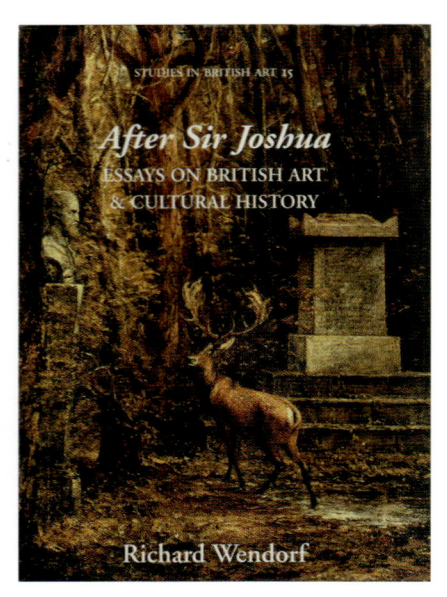

An Inconvenient Revelation

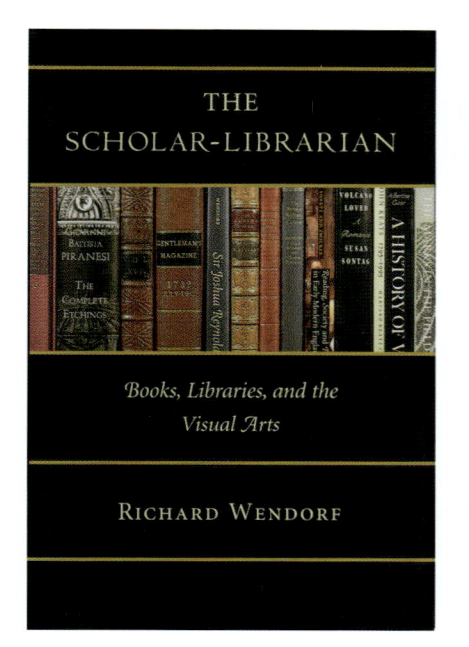

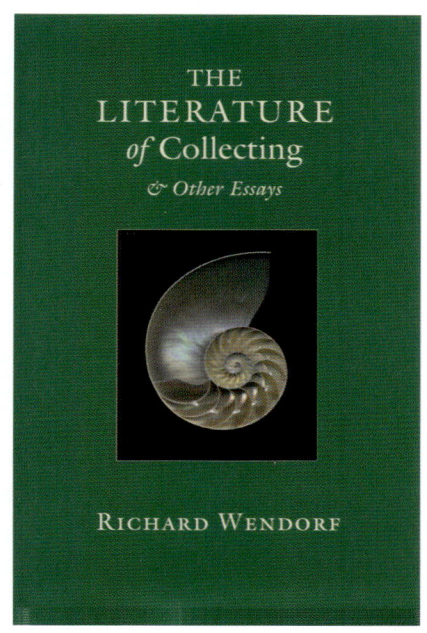

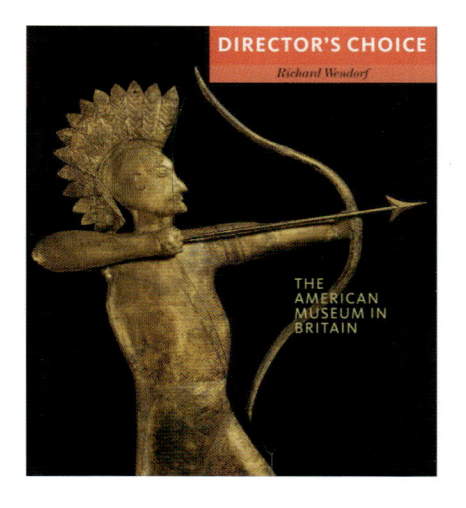

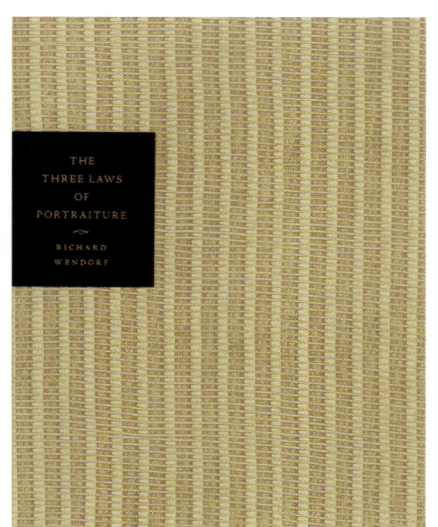

Richard Wendorf

Sir Joshua: Essays on British Art and Cultural History, is still in print, fit testimony not to its popular appeal but to the rather small audience willing to entertain the questions I had attempted to raise.

Throughout the transition I had made between the disciplines of literary criticism and art history, I found myself having to engage with the burgeoning scholarship devoted not just to interrelations between the arts but to the various strands of theory that informed them, especially in the work of Wendy Steiner and W. J. T. Mitchell. But theory, I soon discovered, left me cold. It was essential to master it, to teach it, to draw upon it when it helped to frame an argument, but it remains at a respectful distance from the critical work I find most engaging. I continue to find artistic works, including texts, to be most interesting when I can examine them as material objects. I want to think about the relationship between Piranesi's focus on ancient ruins and the corrosive etching technique that gives his prints their distinctive look. Rossetti has always been an interesting example of the painter who was also a poet (or vice versa, some would say), but he becomes even more interesting, I think, when one can examine the poem written on the frame that surrounds the painting — or, in one important case, the sonnet that is incorporated within the painting itself. Those of us nourished on the relationship between form and function in literary studies should be able to consider the relationship between method and meaning in the visual arts as well.

The scholarly book that I'm currently working on — and have, in fact, been working on for well over a decade — draws many of these strands together, for I'm attempting to chart the emergence of the modern printed page in English. My focus is on the changes in printing conventions that emerged between roughly 1740 and 1770 in London, and my starting point is once again a loose end that I never properly tied up: the transition from a heavily capitalized and italicized edition of William Collins's *Persian Eclogues* in 1742 to the much cleaner, more modern version published fifteen years later. This change has sometimes been called the "great divide" in printing history; I call this transitional process "abandoning the capital." This is by far the most ambitious project I've undertaken, combining the

An Inconvenient Revelation

examination of over 2,000 books (summarized in an electronic database) with comparative studies of French, Italian, Spanish, and early American imprints, explorations of the reading public, manuscript practices, canon formation, the role of printing conventions in the interpretation of texts, and the modern editing of eighteenth-century literature. These changes didn't occur in a vacuum, moreover, and so much of my book's conclusion will be devoted to similar phenomena that occurred at the same time: the publication of Johnson's *Dictionary*, the transition from the Julian to the Gregorian calendar, evolutions in prose style, and quarrels over grammar and shop signs — and even over weights and measures. These are all, in my view, examples of the larger culture's movement towards standardized conventions for ordering the ways in which it does its business and represents itself. But, so far, I have had to settle for correlations among these various strands rather than a strong causal agent. I have not been able to discover anyone in the eighteenth century who has described *why* these changes in printing conventions took place at this particular time. I have a great deal of evidence, but cause and effect are difficult to pin down. I have, in other words, no proverbial smoking gun.

When I finished writing my book on Reynolds, I took a moment to look through all of the notes I had made and the sources and catalogues I had consulted, trying to make sure that I hadn't neglected anything. I was nursing a form of intellectual discomfort, for although I had been able to find numerous examples of how Reynolds was characterized as a pleasing companion and as a painter who pleased his clientele, I couldn't directly attach this "discourse of complaisance" to Reynolds's own utterances or writings. As I looked yet again through a small catalogue of items that Frederick W. Hilles had placed on exhibition at the Beinecke Library many years earlier, I noticed an entry for one of Reynolds's commonplace books. Surely I must have examined it, either at Beinecke or at the Yale Center for British Art, but I couldn't find any evidence that I had done so. So I found out that it was at the British Art Center, made an appointment, and drove to New Haven to take a look. And there it was, in a manuscript that I had somehow missed: an extensive list of quotations that the young Reynolds had copied out on the art of pleasing, many of them from sources (the *Tatler* and *Spectator*, for example) that I had already educed in support of my contention that such a discourse did indeed exist. It was a hallelujah moment — of sorts. For it also reminded me of how close I had come to overlooking the linchpin of my entire argument, and of how embarrassing it would have been if someone running an institution at Harvard were discovered to have neglected the evidence to be found at Yale. But I had it at last: the smoking gun was firmly in my hand.

CHAPTER SIX
Living With Piranesi

In the spring of 1984, as I was slowly resolving to become a better educated and more disciplined print collector, I screwed up my courage and pushed against the thick plate-glass door that led to Stanley Johnson's gallery on Chicago's Michigan Avenue. I had meant to do so for some time, but the gallery looked so elegant, so sophisticated — so grown-up, I suppose — that I had only glimpsed its interior as I was heading in or out of another suite on the second floor of the same building. Stanley himself, as it turned out, was just as forbidding as his gallery: crisp, intense, immaculately tailored, flanked by assistants and a beautiful German wife. The gallery was spare and deserted, and there was no place to hide. Although Stanley's greeting was cordial enough, he was obviously curious about a young stranger who was not nearly as crisp, intense, or immaculately tailored as he was. What was my name? What was I interested in? What could he show me?

On his walls was an exhibition devoted to European printmaking ranging from the work of Dürer and Cranach to that of Bresdin and Picasso. I have never, in the past thirty years, seen a more impressive show outside the walls of a museum, unless (of course) it was in Stanley's own gallery. I attempted to explain that I was very much an amateurish collector, that I had a few prints by Hogarth, but that I was trying to educate my eye (without, I might have added, necessarily flattening my slender wallet). "Hogarth," he exclaimed; yes, there was an engraving by Hogarth in the exhibition, just one (the charming *Strolling Actresses Dressing in a Barn*). Hogarth wasn't a great printmaker, he explained, but he was fun. "Make yourself at home." I pretended to, of course, but as soon as I could take a polite powder I quickly fled.

But I also returned, for the prints on the walls were astonishingly beautiful. Executed by different artists working in different countries at different times and in different media, they nevertheless shared the common representational challenge of working with the brashness or subtlety of black and gray ink on a light and unforgiving ground. Stanley walked me around the gallery and spoke with precision and passion about what made individual images so special: a Goya, a Rosa, a Tiepolo. When we had completed our circuit, he turned to me and delivered the following parable: "If you invited me to visit your apartment, and when I arrived I discovered that you had nothing hanging in your foyer, or in your living room, or in your library — nothing hanging in the dining room, nothing in the corridor — but that you had a small etching by Rembrandt hanging in your bedroom, I would shake you by the hand and say, 'Congratulations! *You* have a first-rate art collection.'"

Advice it was, advice from which both explicit and implicit lessons might be drawn. The generous, explicit moral was that you didn't have to possess many works of art in order to have a collection of integrity and value. The reverse side of Stanley's coin suggested a rather different lesson, however, for it was clear that he preferred empty rooms and bare walls to second-rate works of art. Would he have valued a collection comprising one etching by Rembrandt and several dozen engravings by Hogarth? I doubt it; and my predicament, of course, was that I possessed the Hogarths but not the Rembrandt. To make matters worse, Stanley then asked me what I did for a living. I answered, with what I hoped was hidden satisfaction, that I was a professor of English literature at Northwestern — an eighteenth-century scholar, in fact. Stanley looked as disappointed as anyone I've ever met. "Academics are the worst possible collectors," he replied. "Instead of buying what is beautiful, you invariably buy what you think is interesting."

As I look back on these encounters many years later, I must confess that I have fallen painfully short of Stanley's standards for collecting. My flat in Bath is neat and tidy, but it is also filled with a large number of *things*, very few of which rival the value or beauty of that single Dutch etching hanging in a bedroom in which I shall never sleep. I'm not an undisciplined person; far from it, I'm afraid. But I shall never rival a fastidious colleague of mine who had no furniture at all in his living room because he couldn't afford any of the pieces he approved of.

Living With Piranesi

It is true that I have disposed of all but one of my Hogarths, but the narrow, Spartan path that leads to a single Rembrandt is not for me. I collect what I find to be both interesting *and* attractive, and I take special pleasure in purchasing (and often rehabilitating) what others may have overlooked: a cropped Audubon less valuable than its uncut siblings but more attractive precisely because of its more compact "window"; a smoke-black mezzotint of the painter Benjamin West, rescued from a crumbling frame, crisply matted in white, protected by antique glass and a gold-leaf frame rubbed slightly red; a black-ink drawing almost three feet wide and two feet high that enigmatically fuses a plan and elevation into "A Water Source" (1933), which I am almost certain was modeled by an aspiring English architect after various experiments by Piranesi in the *Antichità Romane*.

How can I be so sure? Because I've lived with Piranesi for the past thirty years. He's to be found almost everywhere in my home, including the bedroom in which I *do* sleep at night. His portrait stares at me in the hallway, his architectural plans-and-elevations are set against the dark taupe walls of a small sitting room, and his son Francesco's *Borghese Gladiator* guards the bedroom for guests. I think that Stanley Johnson might possibly approve, for much of that handsome exhibition in Chicago in 1984 was devoted to Piranesi — almost an entire room, as I now reconstruct it from memory. Never before had I seen such variety from the hand of a single artist. Many of the prints were delicate evocations of a silvery Roman world rendered with a light, almost feathery touch. In stark contrast, other etchings explored the dark nether-world of the *Carceri*, rendered through intense inking and dramatic chiaroscuro. These are the prints that led Marguerite Yourcenar to explore the "dark brain" of Piranesi; these are the images in which my friend Joseph Roach has noted the "chilling paradox" of prisons "to which there are no precise boundaries, yet from which there is no escape."

I was enthralled. There *was* no escape. Piranesi was tantalizingly familiar — in the sense that he was an eighteenth-century artist — but he was simultaneously exotic and remote. He was Italian in the first place, of course, and I knew absolutely nothing about Venice and

Rome in the *Settecento*. I had begun my scholarly career, moreover, by focusing on the ways in which mid-eighteenth-century poetry, particularly the work of William Collins and Thomas Gray, served as a linguistic and cultural bridge between the high Augustan irony of Alexander Pope and the full-blown romanticism of Wordsworth and Coleridge. *My* eighteenth century faced forwards. Piranesi's eighteenth century, on the other hand, was manifestly neoclassical; it looked backwards even when he was envisioning new buildings that might be erected in the Eternal City. Here, then, was a fresh world to explore, a world (as I would eventually discover) that encompassed classical scholarship, architectural history, theatrical scene design, the Grand Tour, and the intricacies of the etching process itself.

But how to begin? I'm certain that Stanley Johnson realized that I couldn't afford the prints in his gallery even before I did. I mentioned my nascent interest to Russell Maylone, the curator of special collections at Northwestern. Had I ever heard of the dealer Letterio Calapai, he asked? Letterio Calapai! The name was too good to be true, and I therefore quickly followed up with a telephone call and a trip north to Glencoe, where Leo (as he was called — and you can imagine why) welcomed me on a chilly Saturday morning. Russell had informed me that Leo was a very distinguished printmaker, much admired by collectors of contemporary art. What Russell didn't tell me (perhaps because he had never put himself in my supplicating position) was that Leo was essentially a print collector rather than a print dealer. He wanted his visitors to appreciate the sheets in his collection; only occasionally, when the spirit (or his bank account) moved him, would he actually sell (perhaps I should say deaccession) one of his prints.

My Saturday morning adventures therefore unfolded in the following manner. The first hour or so would be devoted to admiring Leo's current work, which usually involved a multiple-printing process on a large press in the middle of his studio. Sometimes he would actually be engaged in printing and I would help him move his oversized sheets on and off the press. Then he would share his treasures with me, never mentioning whether any of them might be for sale. Finally, donning my coat and pretending to leave, I would quietly ask if he might be

Living With Piranesi

willing to sell a particular image. The answer was usually no, but he did part with the eight plates of Hogarth's *Rake's Progress*, which I then put to good use in my courses, and Gillray's satirical print of *Titianus Redivivus*, in which the deceased Sir Joshua Reynolds comes back to life in order to discover Titian's secret coloring techniques.

Living with Piranesi proved to be more difficult. Leo certainly owned a good number of them, but they were his particular favorites, and he consulted all the auction catalogues in order to calculate the current value of each etching. Eventually, and with some reluctance, he decided that he would part with one image, a small view of the

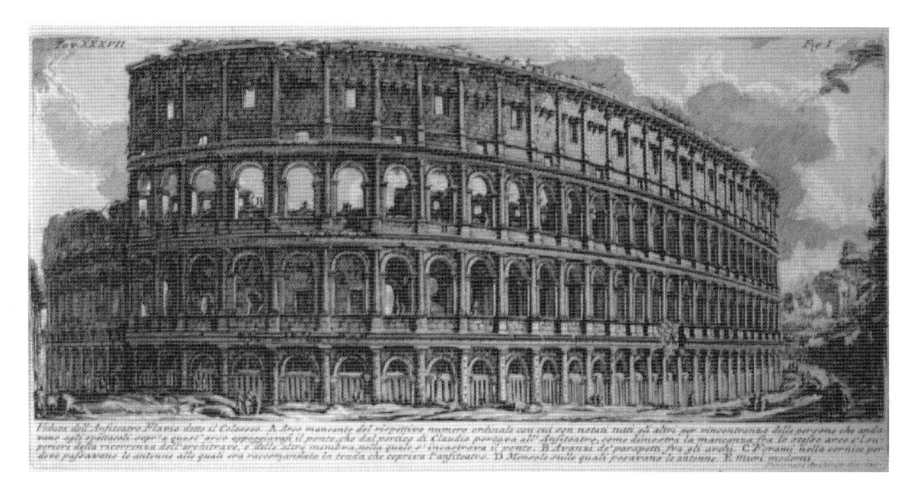

Colosseum from the *Antichità Romane*. It was one of the happiest moments in my life. Later, when I myself deaccessioned the Hogarths and the Gillray, I discovered that, despite Leo's protestations, they were not lifetime impressions. No matter. I had enjoyed them for a long time, had shared them with several generations of students, and could now afford to invest once again in Piranesi. And the *Colosseum*, as it turned out, was "all right" (as my friend Roger Stoddard likes to phrase it). I bought a decent frame and proudly displayed the etching as the only object sitting on my mantelpiece. It wasn't a Rembrandt, but it *was* a beginning.

Now that I was properly launched, I gradually introduced myself to various print dealers in England as well as in America. There were quite a few at the time, even in Chicago, and I soon became friends with David Gee, who worked out of a wonderfully ramshackle apartment and studio perched at the top of a building on North Wells Street. Like Leo Calapai, David turned out to be a collector who would occasionally sell prints he actually valued himself: not the Piranesi in the bedroom, of course, nor the portrait of Giambattista that hung in his studio, but eventually a lovely, small etching by Legros that I bought precisely because it was beautiful rather than interesting.

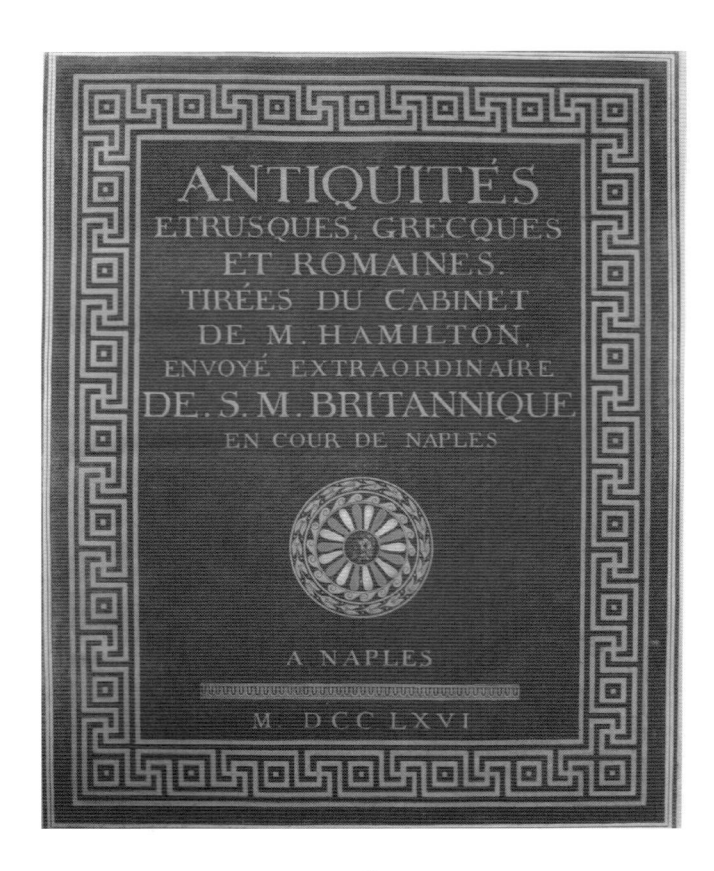

Much more to my nascent taste for the neoclassical was an intriguing title-page to one of the four volumes devoted to Sir William Hamilton's collection of antique vases. Handsomely printed in black and then hand-colored using terracotta-tinted wash, the title-page was one of eight plates, four in French and four in English, that introduced readers to the sumptuous volumes produced for Hamilton by the self-styled Baron d'Hancarville. I had already seen several of the engravings of the Greek and Etruscan vases themselves, but not the striking title-pages with their dramatic Greek-key motifs within the elaborate borders. David loved the print just as much as I did; would he part with it? Eventually, yes; who else, after all, could possibly share his interest in such an unusual image? And it didn't hurt that I was a fellow Iowan, willing to listen to David talk about his early years in rural America. David was also a conservator, mat-cutter, and framer, and thus my eight Hogarths were entrusted to him along with the Hamiltonian singleton. Many years later I discovered all *eight* of the title-pages, in pristine condition, in a small gallery in London. They had been consigned to the attic because, as the incredulous dealer told me, "we didn't think anyone would be interested in buying them."

If you have followed my tale this far, you can surely discern a pattern beginning to emerge. Because I didn't have the capital to walk into a gallery like Stanley Johnson's and choose from among a variety of beautiful impressions, I had — of necessity — begun to develop alternative sources in the marketplace of art. Leo and David did not think of themselves as dealers; one was an artist, the other was a paper conservator, and both were collectors. But a good deal of patience and an interest in their own work occasionally secured me prints that I couldn't otherwise afford. In addition, of course, I had everything to learn — about the market as well as the prints themselves — and my conversations with both men gave me genuine pleasure, for we shared a passion that appealed to few fellow-travelers. This is not to say that I was bottom-fishing, as they say in the real-estate market. My goal was not to buy low and sell high, but rather to establish a corpus of good impressions of Piranesi's work by purchasing the best images available at a reasonable price. Some dealers, moreover, turned out to be affordable, particularly in London, which boasted a number of shops devoted to old-master prints twenty years ago: Craddock and

Barnard, Schuster, Sotheran (in two locations), Christopher Mendez, and Robert Douwma and Ben Weinreb (sometimes together, sometimes apart). Only Sotheran, alas, still exists as a shop in London.

Like many collectors in the early stages of their careers, I began by trying to find representative images of an artist's major works. In Piranesi's case, this meant the large etchings of Roman views, the *vedute* he continued to produce throughout his lifetime. I found one (a really splendid impression) at an antiques show in Chicago; I later purchased a second from Christopher Mendez and eventually a third from Sotheran. Then, in 1986, when I was attending the exhibition and symposium devoted to Sir Joshua Reynolds at the Royal Academy in London, I discovered that Ben Weinreb was offering what seemed like *all* of Piranesi in a new gallery located behind the British Museum: 193 prints as well as the entire *Antichità Romane* in four volumes. This turned out to be an unnerving (and, eventually, a backbone-stiffening) event, for it was possible to choose from all of the major series: the *Prima Parte*, the *Vedute di Roma*, the *Opere Varie*, the four *Grotteschi*, and the late, dark etchings devoted to the ruins at Paestum.

With virtually all of Piranesi's world lying open before me, how was I to choose? I made two important decisions that afternoon. First, realizing that I could *just* afford a copy of one of the more important *vedute* from the early nineteenth-century Paris edition but *not* one from the contemporary editions printed in Rome, I decided to wait, to defer — perhaps the most painful decision a collector ever makes, for collectors are rarely connoisseurs of delayed gratification. I realized, however, that the advice I had received from Stanley should be brought into play at this point. Lifetime impressions of Piranesi's work are appreciably superior to the copies his son Francesco printed after he moved to Paris and became François; this was one of the visible lessons such a comprehensive exhibition could easily instill. And so I decided to collect only etchings printed before Piranesi's death in 1778. It was not, after all, a case of not being able to display any furniture in my living room, for there were many other prints, from many other series, from which to choose.

My other decision that cold February afternoon might not so eas-

Living With Piranesi

ily have pleased Stanley Johnson. Realizing, as I surveyed the scores of prints on the walls, that *everything* seemed beautiful to me, I decided to purchase what I found most interesting. I already had a small Colosseum, so to speak, and three handsome *vedute*, why not begin to be as experimental in my collecting as Piranesi himself was in his printmaking? And thus began the second phase in my life as a collector as I turned my attention to frontispieces, title-pages, and initial letters, an interest already whetted by my painstakingly slow acquisition of the odd "Hamilton" and conveniently aided and abetted by my own work as a literary scholar. In addition to several conventional etchings from the *Antichità Romane*, I therefore left the gallery with an impression of Piranesi's title-page to the *Prima Parte* of 1743, his first collection of prints to be issued in codex form.

The odd title-page, frontispiece, and *letterina* followed, and then — several years later — I took a third step as a *collecteur piranesien* by purchasing a number of large architectural subjects that combine plan, elevation, and various legends and inscriptions in an unusual format. It might be said that title-pages and studies of capital roman letters break the traditional (and naïve) illusion of artistic realism by introducing elements from two complementary (or competing) semiotic systems: one linguistic, the other more purely visual. The linguistic element is usually subordinate, embedded within the larger visual field but also contributing to it. In the title-page to the *Prima Parte*, for instance, the figures near the center of the etching are pointing to letters that have almost entirely disappeared. In Piranesi's studies of initial letters, the capital "N" or "L" or "S" is the center of the viewer's focus, but the letter is rendered as an architectural element, part of a larger ensemble within the visual field.

In the etchings that combine plans and elevations as well as inscriptions and legends, Piranesi takes this assault on "realistic" printmaking one step further. It is impossible — or at least exceedingly difficult — to read an inscription while simultaneously perceiving the entire image within which it is embedded. It is correspondingly impossible — or at least exceedingly difficult — to study a plan and an elevation at the same time. When these two forms of competing discourse are then combined in the same image, Piranesi's viewers are required to undertake an even more complicated process of interpretation. The image can no longer be "taken in" at one time, or from one perspective, as was the case with the diminutive Colosseum. Different semiotic elements demand different "ways of looking" that must then be integrated in order to make sense of the complexity (and playfulness) of Piranesi's designs.

Forced to turn out the beautiful but conventional *vedute* throughout his lifetime in order to make a proper living as an artist, Piranesi might be thought to have turned to these other, highly unusual compilations as a welcome form of experimentation and release. Unless, of course, we look even more closely at those etchings that I've characterized as conventional, for Piranesi is full of surprises. His

Living With Piranesi

first collected etchings, in the *Prima Parte*, may appear at first glance to be straightforward renderings of classical ruins and neoclassical buildings, but they are in fact designs for structures that have not yet been built (even though some of them have already decayed). Each *veduta* contains a cartouche, usually found at the bottom edge of the plate block, which contains information about the buildings depicted above. These are semantic enclaves, visually separated from the mimetic image; but they often take the form of an architectural fragment, and they always contain letters (A, B, C, D) that can also be found in the image proper. (It would be difficult, in fact, to find an etching by Piranesi that did not contain lettering of one kind or another, and some of his title-pages and dedications contain almost nothing *but* carved inscriptions.) In some examples, as in the *Veduta dell'avanzo del Portico di M. Emilio Lepido*, from the *Antichità Romane*, the cartouche actually breaks through the lower edge of the picture, puncturing the otherwise realistic illusion of the etching and even casting a shadow on the lettering below.

Richard Wendorf

The kinds of images that I have acquired in this third phase of collecting can therefore be thought of as Piranesi's even more radical attempts to explore the visual syntax of the plate block. That he took self-conscious delight in exploding conventions and poking fun at traditional illusionism can be gauged, at least in part, by his penchant for presenting so many of these elements as prints-within-prints, as curling documents pinned to other documents. Some of these images, as in the *Pars cellarum subterranearum Capitolii* from the *Campo Marzio*,

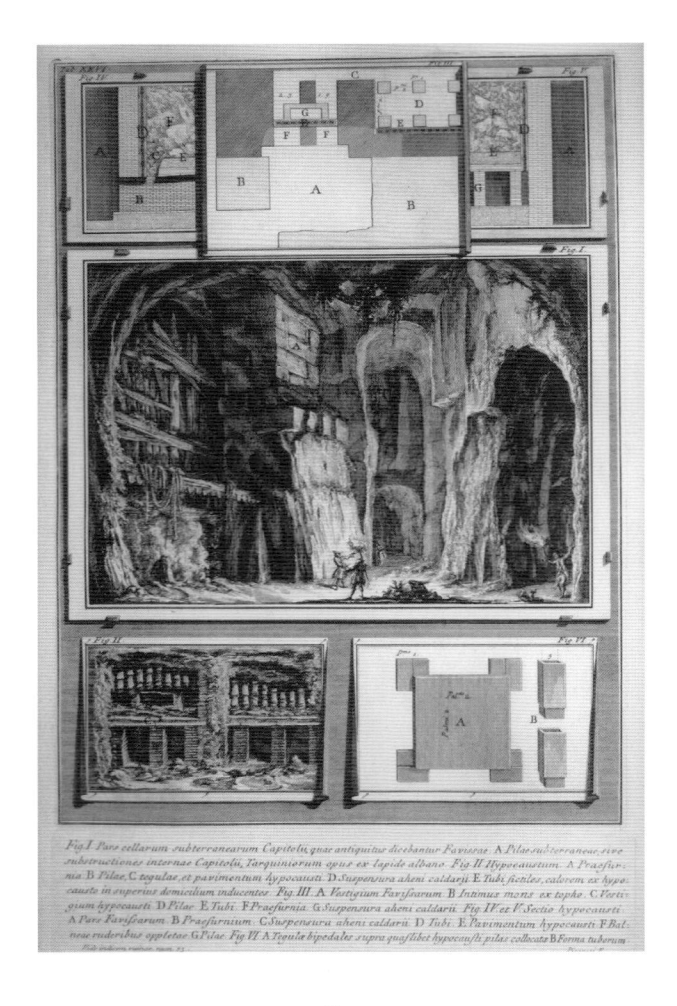

Living With Piranesi

which I discovered at a local antiques show outside of Boston, suggest that the etching is not so much devoted to certain buildings as it is to the props and paraphernalia of architectural practice. Doomed to be an architect *manqué*, with only a few projects to his credit, Piranesi could nonetheless re-create the texture of an architect's life both in the subject of his etchings and in their self-referentiality.

The frustration of living in Rome at a moment when great architectural commissions could not be had must have been particularly galling to someone with Piranesi's talent and pride. It is therefore not surprising that, by all accounts, he was not a person with whom it was easy to live. A jealous husband, a demanding father, an irascible polemicist, he was quite adept at biting the hand of the patron who fed him. We are much more fortunate today, now that the passion and the overarching ambition have been distilled into the silvery tones produced by paper, ink, and copperplate. Aristocrats, he once noted, are the latest in their lineage whereas artists are the first in theirs. Piranesi clearly understood his place in the history of printmaking as he forsook his draftsman's pencil for the etching needle.

One of the virtues, and pleasures, of living with Piranesi today is that the images themselves speak so eloquently on his behalf. In saying this, I am not referring to the inscriptional elements in his prints so much as his ability to engage his viewers in the process of interpretation. I have felt this most strongly as I have pondered the forces at work in the intriguing title-page to the *Prima Parte*. For a long time I took simple enjoyment in speculating about these shadowy figures as they gesticulated on my living-room wall. What were they pointing to? Why was the large marble tablet near the center of the composition partially obscured by a low, rolling mist?

Following the publication of Andrew Robison's magisterial catalogue of the early imaginative "fantasies," however, I suddenly realized that the print I owned was in fact the fourth state of the first edition — and that the first and second states presented dramatically different images. Why, I then asked myself, did Piranesi only introduce human figures in later states of the etching? And why did these figures emerge only when the engraved inscription on the marble tablet began to disappear? I articulated my answers to these questions in an exploratory essay entitled "Piranesi's Double Ruin," and in doing so I began to speculate as well about the particular affinity between the subject of so much of Piranesi's work (his predilection for representing buildings in ruinous states) and the corrosive nature of the etching process itself. If I have made any contribution at all to the critical understanding of Piranesi's achievement as an artist, it lies, I believe, in my insistence on linking the physical process and aesthetic effects of etching with Piranesi's lifelong interest in the decay and dissemination of classical culture.

Once I had published "Piranesi's Double Ruin," I sent copies of the essay to several of the print dealers who had befriended me in recent years. One of them, Michael Finney — whose eponymous gallery used to be found on Museum Street in London — asked if I would like to examine a print he had recently purchased: "it's a dirty thing, but *you* might find it interesting," as he playfully put it. And indeed I did, even though I couldn't immediately determine what it actually was. Once I had recourse to Robison's catalogue and to some helpful magnification, however, I realized that the "dirty" sheet was a scratch-proof impression of one of the plates added to the *Prima Parte* late in the 1740s. What I had in my hands, in other words, was one of Piranesi's rare working copies of a print-in-progress — his "foul paper," so to speak, complete with the prick holes indicating that he had pinned it to a board or easel as he calibrated the lettering at the bottom of the print. The second state of this etching devoted to the elaborate, imaginary interior of an ancient temple would in time become one of Piranesi's most influential designs, and I was delighted a few months later when I discovered a beautiful impression of it in Russ Gerard's gallery on Charles Street, just a few blocks from the Boston Athenæum. All I now lack, of course, is a copy of the first state before the lettering, a print that I still hope to find someday.

The proof-sheet that now hangs next to the second state of the *Tempio antico* is a dirty thing indeed; it would certainly be out of place in a Madison (or Michigan) Avenue gallery, and that's fine with me. Foul papers, like sleeping dogs, shouldn't be disturbed. It's comforting, after all, to know that these odd remnants from the printing house have actually survived after two and a half centuries. Walter Benjamin's sense of the "aura" surrounding original or unique artifacts is rather too grand a conception to impose on such a slight survivor, but the scratch-proof impression nevertheless brings us a step closer to the material world in which Piranesi worked as an etcher.

So, of course, do the surviving drawings from Piranesi's hand, most of them now housed in great institutional collections. I have only acquired two drawings myself — neither, of course, by Piranesi: a fine but anonymous rendering of a bust of Homer, probably a statue in the collection of the Royal Academy at the close of the eighteenth century; and a watercolor by the Scottish artist Frances Stoddart, whose painting of a similar scene hangs over my breakfast table. Piranesi's own drawings rarely appear in the auction houses, and when they do they naturally fetch prices well beyond the reach of ordinary collectors such as I. With the exception of the detailed designs executed near the end of his life at Paestum, Piranesi's drawings tend to be rather unfinished. "I realize that the complete drawing isn't on my drawing paper," he confessed to his fellow *ruiniste* Hubert Robert; "however, it is very much in my head and you will see it in its entirety on my etching plate." His advice was to "go slowly," for in producing one etching "I am really in the midst of executing three thousand drawings all at the same time."

Johann Winckelmann, who argued at such length with Piranesi over the origins of Roman culture, believed that "just as the first pressing of the grapes gives the most exquisite wine, so the . . . sketch on paper of the draughtsman affords us the true spirit of the artist." I also admire and enjoy the work of great draftsmen, but I do so on aesthetic rather than vaguely metaphysical grounds. Charles Ryskamp assembled a remarkable collection of drawings, a collection rich in quality as well as range. But any collection of drawings — or of paintings, for that matter — strikes me as somewhat promiscuous in comparison with the clarity and chasteness I value in old-master prints.

Some of my friends take a very different view of this matter, to say the least. Why, they sometimes ask, can't I introduce a little more color onto the walls? My answer, of course, is that we should paint the walls, not the art. But living with me, after all, is probably even more difficult than living with Giambattista, and living with both of us is certainly not for the faint of heart. Whatever collecting is — avocation, aspiration, sublimation, illness, grounds for divorce or disinheritance — it is also one of the most significant ways in which we

Living With Piranesi

express the values by which we live. I, for one, continue to count myself fortunate that I had the temerity, three decades ago, to push past the plate-glass door and sample the treasures within.

CHAPTER SEVEN
The Petrified Mouse

In the summer of 1989, just a few weeks before I was to forsake Chicago for the banks of the Charles, my friends Helen and Michael Goodkin hosted a small but festive party on my behalf. I had been a professor and a dean, and I was soon to become a library director; wasn't it about time I met some proper librarians, they kindly asked? I found one of their guests to be particularly interesting, as virtually everyone did when meeting Robert Rosenthal for the first time. He was the legendary proprietor of the special collections department at the University of Chicago, someone who ran his shop the old-fashioned way — and ran it well. Serving an apprenticeship with him was a much-coveted experience, for Bob possessed a marvelous sense of humor as well as a profound knowledge of rare books and manuscripts. I learned, for example, that he had formed a tontine to collect books published in the year 1900. According to Terry Belanger, the "three members of the group were Michael Turner (then head of special collections at the Bodleian), Rosenthal, and myself," but only Rosenthal took the project seriously, discovering a cheap copy of the *Cumulative Book Index* for 1900 almost the day after the trio first made their unusual compact.

Near the end of the evening, Bob took me aside and confided that he had a small anecdote to share with me, something that I might find useful once I had made my way to the Houghton Library. It was actually an academic joke, one that he had probably heard many years ago. Here's how it goes:

> There once was a man who had two sons — identical twins — whom he simply couldn't tell apart. When they turned eighteen, he therefore decided to send one to New Haven to become a rowdy and the other to Cambridge to become a gentleman. True to form, one

The Petrified Mouse

son became a Yale rowdy and the other a Harvard gentleman, but when they returned to their father following their graduation, he still couldn't tell them apart.

During my eight years at Harvard, I told this joke many times and always to good effect. No one seemed to have heard it before, everyone found it amusing, and everyone appeared to find it amusing in his or her own particular way. For some, the point was that a rowdy at Yale is essentially the same thing as a gentleman at Harvard. For others, the joke affirmed what many believe but rarely admit, which is that august institutions such as Yale and Harvard don't really have that much influence on the young men and women who enter their gates. For still others, the moral was even more general, which is that certain gentlemen are in fact rowdy and that certain men who try to be rowdy are — no matter how hard they try — still very much gentlemen. Each time I finished telling this joke, there was a slight interval (perhaps only the proverbial nanosecond) before the first ripple of laughter began, and then a continuing rumble of approval as the intricacy of the tale finally took hold.

During my career as a library director at Harvard, I drew upon this fable both to break the ice at the beginning of a talk and, more importantly, to remind those who view the world through crimson-colored glasses that the university (and its libraries) are not in fact unique: older, larger, and richer perhaps, but not unlike other American institutions in a number of important ways. Space restrictions, the preservation and conservation of collections, the challenges and promises of technology, changing patterns in scholarship, limited resources, greater visibility (and perceived accessibility) within the larger community — all of these are important and often pressing issues that confront every research library in America, and Harvard is no exception. The oldest, largest, and richest university library in the United States might even be thought of as the progenitor of many of its competitors, the model from which the blueprint for academic library systems has been so successfully (and expensively) implemented. Without Houghton, for instance, there would arguably be no rowdy Beinecke at Yale, let alone an even rowdier Ransom Humanities Center in Texas, both of which are now richer (and perhaps larger) than their hardscrabble cousin in Cambridge. The fundamental point I therefore had the temerity to make, first at Harvard and then to sympathetic audiences outside the university, was that the Houghton Library had a good deal to learn from (as well as to contribute to) the wider library community.

At first glance it appeared to me, moreover, that "haughty" Houghton was showing its age. The climate-control system, which had been state-of-the-art when the library opened its doors in 1942, was very much in need of renovation in 1989. The books and manuscripts were catalogued in four different places in three different buildings, and there was no plan for a retrospective conversion of the catalogue cards to electronic form. The stacks were full and 40 percent of the manuscripts had not been catalogued. Planning had not begun for the library's fiftieth anniversary, which was to be celebrated in less than three years. When I tried to set up my computer in my

The Petrified Mouse

new and rather grand office, I discovered that there were no three-pronged electrical outlets there. Later in the same day I discovered that my secretary, who had announced her departure a few weeks before I arrived, was the only staff member who had a computer for other than cataloguing purposes; everyone else used a typewriter or wrote letters by hand.

I also learned that my new position was not necessarily a comfortable one in other respects. My immediate predecessor had been translated to Widener; *his* predecessor had taken early retirement, consoling himself by teaching bibliography courses in the English department. The recent chair of that department told me that his colleagues referred to Houghton as "the mausoleum." The current chair of the English department told me that Houghton was essentially an obsolete institution; none of his professorial colleagues would darken our doors. The "archive," he kindly informed me, consisted not of books and manuscripts in special collections libraries, but of a handful of seminal theoretical texts, which varied from scholar to scholar. The College Librarian, Y. T. Feng (to whom I reported), confessed that she would not be able to make me the associate librarian for special collections, which she had promised to do when I was being recruited: "What would the heads of the other special libraries think?" The Director of the Harvard University Library, Sidney Verba, was fond of saying, as a form of compliment, that "we threw Richard straight into the deep end, and he came right back up to the surface." It was not an auspicious beginning.

It was not my life's ambition, as you can imagine, to dogpaddle in troubled waters, but it *was* important to examine the circumstances that produced such metaphors. I had never worked, or studied, or lived anywhere before where intelligent people actually explained that things were done in a certain manner "because they've always been done that way." One incident in particular will illustrate my predicament. Soon after I arrived at Houghton, a colleague came into my office late one afternoon to inform me that something serious had been discovered in the stacks. I asked what it was. "A mouse," I was told. Dead or alive, I asked? "Dead." Recently dead, I asked, or dead for some time? "Oh, dead for some time. It's petrified." I thanked my colleague for this information, but he did not leave. I asked what the matter was. "Is it all right to dispose of the mouse?" Of course, I answered; why did he ask? "Because nothing in the Houghton Library is to be discarded without the permission of the Librarian."

I was used to working in a university that looked forward and outward; I now found myself attempting to flourish in one that often seemed to look backward and inward. I was used to living in a city that, without ignoring its own extraordinary history, had its eye clearly focused on where it was headed. I now lived in a city that sometimes appeared to be obsessed with where it came from and often suspicious of changes that would alter that precious status quo. I was told again and again how pleased I must be to have moved from Chicago, usually by people whom I was fairly sure had never set foot there. Instead of answering them directly, I usually replied that Chicago was a metropolitan city, whereas Boston was cosmopolitan — a mischievous response that somehow seemed to get me off the hook.

It did not help, moreover, that Houghton was perceived as being not just special but somehow aloof: a mausoleum to the professoriate, perhaps, but an aristocratic establishment in the minds of many of our colleagues in Harvard's other libraries. Our senior cataloguer, Hugh Amory, characterized these distinctions in architectural terms.

> Rare book libraries come in three varieties: the familiar temple, a form they share with public libraries; the corporate headquarters, specimens of which may be seen in the Beinecke Library or the Humanities Research Center in Austin; and the private house, as in the Morgan or the Huntington. At Harvard, Widener is the Parish Church, and Houghton is the Manor House. The social implications of this are not lost on our readers.

Nor, I should add, on one's fellow librarians — or on the general public, should anyone actually be tempted to visit us. It was one thing to point out that Houghton (unlike Widener) did not charge visiting scholars for access to its collections, but it was quite another thing to combat the general perception that the library was essentially an elitist institution. Comments like David Nyhan's in the *Boston Globe* didn't make matters any better. Writing on behalf of a beleaguered television program entitled "The 10 O'clock News," Nyhan confessed that "at times it could be so arch, so fey, so prissy, so unremittingly correct, you'd choke. It's like the Houghton Library at Harvard; not for everybody, sure, but it's damned important there is at least one of its kind hereabouts." With friends like these, one hardly needed enemies.

The challenge, of course, was to be "correct" — to be shrewd, wise, thoughtful, enterprising — without being either prissy or fey. But how to begin? An important first step consisted in persuading our colleagues in the university that we were a welcoming institution. Generations of undergraduates had been put off by the sight of this neo-Georgian manor house situated near the center of Harvard

Yard; it was time to invite them in. We did so by encouraging faculty members in the humanities and social sciences to consider including Houghton's materials in their assignments, and even to teach their seminars within our walls. I offered to speak to each department; when I did, I discovered that there was genuine interest in putting our resources to work as well as considerable surprise that we were willing to reach out to constituencies that had long felt neglected. Within a relatively short time, certainly in less than two years, we were almost the victims of our own success as professors in various departments asked to hold their classes within the library. In order to emphasize our new role, I had the old wooden doors replaced by clear glass, which was the most dramatic physical gesture we could make in the direction of demystification and inclusiveness.

Just as important was our effort to work together with "the Wadsworths and the Wideners," as one of my associates referred to the university and college librarians. My colleagues and I took on more committee assignments, served on more search committees, and joined the queue to implement a strategic planning process deep in the bowels of haughty Houghton. I agreed to run the Fine Arts Library for almost a year. In return, we were included in Harvard's massive retrospective conversion project as well as in the planning and use of the new depository library system — the much-emulated "HD." Once our fiftieth anniversary was upon us (in 1992), we were able to celebrate by looking forward as well as through the rear-view mirror. Three exhibitions and their catalogues paid appropriate tribute to Harvard's rare book and manuscript collections, and to the librarians who brought them to Cambridge. But the year concluded with a symposium devoted to the future of special collections libraries, with speakers drawn from across the country as well as Europe. Once the proceedings had been edited and published, we sent a copy to every faculty member in the humanities and social sciences, hoping that our newly cultivated core constituency would realize that the local manor house was attempting to put its imprint on the wider world of libraries once again.

As I now look back, with some hindsight, on my time at Harvard, I am keenly aware of what we could not — or simply did not — achieve. But I can also take a certain amount of satisfaction in reminding myself of how much we actually did accomplish, and of how many of my colleagues joined forces to make Houghton a more modern and lively institution. This is not to say that we didn't encounter difficulties at many a turn. Much energy had to be devoted to rearguard actions that would protect the library's budget and thus the size of its staff, especially during financially troubled times. I had hoped to make these efforts as invisible as possible, for I did not want my colleagues to know how hard — and how often — we were pressed; but I'm certain that many of them fully understood our situation, having experienced similar difficulties long before I joined them. I began to realize how cyclical these financial forces could be even during the eight years of my directorship. A university as old and large and rich as Harvard could not entirely insulate its diverse constituencies from external conditions, especially the severe recession that followed the dubious "Massachusetts miracle" of the late 1980s.

Even in moments of adversity, moreover, it was important to recall the fable of the despairing father and his identical twins. Harvard (and Houghton) were not unique; other libraries were suffering or expanding or fine-tuning themselves during the 1990s. Everything we pursued was essentially in step with the aspirations of our sibling institutions. If we could occasionally demonstrate leadership in one form or another, so much the better; but if other libraries provided an attractive model (as Beinecke did with its extensive visiting-fellowship program), that was fine too. And so we completed the retrospective conversion of our book records and began to automate the records for manuscripts, prints, photographs, playbills, and other works on paper. We renovated the climate-control system, the storage areas for photographs and architectural plans, and the reading room and its environs. (Perhaps my gravestone should read, "He removed the water from the Houghton Library and put it back in the Boston Athenæum.") We raised the funding for twelve visiting fellowships and for professional development opportunities for staff members as well. Typewriters began to disappear; members of the English department began to darken our (transparent glass) doors; and *Rare Book and Manuscript Libraries in the Twenty-First Century* became, fittingly, a collectable book in its own right. The manuscript collection was still 40 percent uncatalogued when I left, but that's another story, and essentially a success story at that, given the continuing dedication of my colleagues.

In the course of charting what were, for me, entirely new waters, I began to formulate a number of propositions about special collections libraries and the environments in which they operate. Grounded in my experience as an observer — as an academic *flâneur*, within my own and other institutions — these formulations were meant not so much to predict outcomes as to provoke discussion about where we were headed. I began by floating the paradoxical proposition that *the traditional library is not what it used to be*, that it can embrace prevalent forms of change without necessarily losing sight of the singularity of its identity and history.

Libraries will always be engaged in, or at least actively contemplating, changes in the way they fulfill their missions. The nature of those missions may also change, as we have seen most dramatically in the evolution of public libraries into full-service institutions within the community, offering amenities to an increasingly diverse clientele that now ranges from preschoolers to senior citizens. Traditional libraries — by which I mean institutions, like Houghton, with a strong focus on books, manuscripts, and the artistic and mechanical processes that produced them — do not pose an exception to this rule. Rare book libraries, membership libraries, and historical societies face many of the same constraints and opportunities as do their larger and more comprehensive counterparts. But when they are challenged, for example, by the advent of electronic technology, their response will be to harness it — to put it to the best possible use — and to place it in the proper perspective.

Technology should be a familiar subject to us, after all; it lies at the heart of printing and book history. The most recent revolution, dazzling as it may appear in its purported transformation of how we pursue knowledge and communicate with each other, is only the third of three. The first technological revolution, the invention of writing, continues to dwarf in importance both the development of moveable type in the mid-fifteenth century and the reconstruction of the world in bits and bytes near the close of the twentieth. A digitized image of a medieval manuscript or an early modern book may both widen and sharpen the educational process, but it cannot wholly substitute for the experience of examining the original object, or for the experience of learning from those whose job it is to pass on their hard-earned knowledge of how and why these cultural artifacts were made. Similarly, the growth of "content" on the web, extraordinary as it is, makes the *interpretation* of so much information all the more crucial. In the long run, there is still much to be said for the primal encounter between critical judgment, on the one hand, and the full spectrum of cultural production, in all of its formats, on the other.

If the traditional library is no longer what it used to be (now that it has passed through the crucible of an electronic revolution), that doesn't mean that it's no longer traditional, at least in the best senses of that long-suffering word: not unduly focused on its past, on the way things have always been done, but not forsaking its core audience and central mission as it strives to harness technology and accommodate other forms of change. I therefore felt comfortable in arguing that *almost everything we prize about our current institutions will have a place in the library of the future* — at least in the near future. The construction of websites and the digitization of texts and images are certainly not incompatible with a more traditional focus on interpretive programs — lectures, exhibitions, publications, teaching out of the collections — that have been the hallmark of so many rare book libraries during the past several decades. Many central library activities, moreover (I am thinking of acquisitions, cataloguing, and reference services in particular), have already been significantly enhanced by the advent of the new technology; doubtless others will follow. Enhancement strikes me as both the most realistic and the most promising way to characterize what technology has in store for us.

The nature of the materials we collect will continue to evolve, moreover, partly because of what is available (and affordable) in the marketplace, partly because of changing patterns in scholarship. I can't imagine the great research libraries failing to strengthen their central collections whenever they can: type specimens and writing books at the Newberry Library, old-master drawings and illuminated manuscripts at the Morgan, or Western Americana and early English historical papers at the Huntington. But certain new scholarly patterns have clearly emerged, particularly in the study of women, gender, sexual practices and preferences, African-American literature and history, and colonial and post-colonial history and literature. Several generations of American scholars have now heeded Mikhail Bakhtin's maxim that "the most intense and productive life of culture takes place on the boundaries." The margins have now become central to the study of art, literature, and history — a development, by the way, that makes "universal" libraries as well as unpruned specialist collections look all the more prescient.

It can be difficult to know which boundaries to explore, however, and it is sometimes easy to make costly mistakes. Houghton's founding librarian, the formidable Bill Jackson, had no trouble in pursuing copies of early English books listed (or, better yet, unlisted) in Wing and the STC, and he was remarkably successful in convincing New Englanders to rid their attics of the seminal documents of the American Renaissance. But his decision to build a modernist collection around the Sitwell family has not sat well, so to speak, with later generations of curators and scholars. The challenge during my own tenure was to build upon the library's great British and American collections by developing a more international focus on contemporary writing. We were therefore cultivating New Directions and the *New Republic* with one hand while we were purchasing the manuscripts of Wole Soyinka and Chinua Achebe with the other. I was particularly interested in acquiring V. S. Naipaul's papers for Harvard, for I believed — and still do believe — that while his work is uneven, he best personifies the forces at play in contemporary culture. A writer of Indian descent raised in the Caribbean and living in England, Naipaul has trained an often scathing eye on Africa and the Americas as well as the sub-continent. We had a cordial lunch in London; I made what, for Houghton, was an unprecedented offer; but we were badly outbid by the University of Tulsa, a telling reminder of how many rivals Harvard now had.

In the long run, of course, I don't think it makes any great difference whether Naipaul's papers are in Tulsa or Cambridge; the important thing is that they are in safe keeping, properly catalogued, and accessible to the scholarly world. Competition is healthy, and no one — not even the Getty — can afford to be complacent. By collecting Achebe and Soyinka and trying to corner the market in Naipaul, we were in fact following the shrewd advice proffered by Stanley Katz during our fiftieth-anniversary symposium. Noting that rare book libraries are usually located at the center of university campuses, Katz predicted that the challenge will lie in bringing them to the center intellectually as well. Reconceptualized special collections libraries and librarians can emerge, he argued in 1992, "as significant and creative elements in the reconfigured university of the next century. Ironically, the rare books operation may move from the snob periphery to the intellectual core of the university as it behaves less as inventory than as utility, as it becomes more intellectually proactive in its behavior."

The more successfully a rare book library moves from the periphery, the more likely it is to *experience a dramatic increase — a virtual explosion — in the use of its materials.* Part of this increased demand has already been generated by unprecedented access through retrospective conversion and the growth of national bibliographic utilities, but part has almost certainly been fueled by the rise in interdisciplinary scholarship and by a renewed emphasis on research in the undergraduate curriculum. Special collections libraries can also move toward the center by taking responsibility for a wider range of historical objects. In Houghton's case, the traditional cut-off date for the automatic transfer of older books found in the stacks of Widener was 1700; by the time I left we had moved that date to 1820, roughly the end of the hand-press era, substantially enlarging our book stock and thereby increasing the conservation and preservation needs of our collections.

Progress comes at a cost. Of course it does, and not simply in financial terms, daunting as they may be. Librarians themselves will have to be part of the program. When I was involved in the extensive interviewing process before I was offered the librarianship of Houghton, I was asked a fundamental (and plangent) question by one of the curators: "What exactly are we supposed to do these days?" In years past, he explained, he had acquired materials for the library and made sure that they were properly catalogued. Now he was supposed to serve on committees, give presentations, teach courses, prepare exhibitions, and raise the money to make all of these additional activities happen. Was the acquisitions program still important? How were librarians to set priorities for themselves and their departments? How could each of these responsibilities be carried out with the care and integrity that Harvard required of its curatorial staff, that "shadow faculty" which added so much to the richness of a student's educational experience?

I had no easy answers then and few comforting answers by the time I departed. As one of my colleagues in human resources bluntly put it, "No one owns his or her own job description." Libraries are organic entities; they need to change — intelligently, carefully — if they are to survive, let alone flourish. Those who enjoy the privilege of serving in these institutions should no longer count on working within a quaint time-warp. Virtually all rare book and manuscript libraries, moreover, are at the mercy of regional as well as national economies. In Terry Belanger's shrewd formulation, each represents a national treasure that must be supported by local resources, and even the most formidable of endowments can shrink. But local resources can sometimes prove to be quite surprising, and I was occasionally pleased to learn, after failing to find external sources of funding, how many forms of support existed within the university itself. In the case of old, large, and rich Harvard, perhaps this should not actually be so surprising. Often, I discovered, an institution with a certain amount of critical mass simply attracts other resources to it, as if some arcane law of cultural astrophysics were at play. Working in such a hothouse environment was often difficult, to say the least. One of my recently hired colleagues tearfully complained to me that

The Petrified Mouse

"Harvard has so many rules, and none of them are written down!" I entirely understood his predicament, but even though I continued to think of myself as an odd man out, at the end of eight years I felt that I had slowly, finally learned how to play the game.

CHAPTER EIGHT

Self-Portrait With Donors

NEAR THE conclusion of my time at the Houghton Library, the curator of manuscripts, Rodney Dennis, and I received an inquiry about our possible interest in a long-missing part of a letter from John Keats to his brother George and sister-in-law Georgiana in the Kentucky wilderness. Scholars had long had a version of this lengthy and important letter, which runs to sixty pages on thirty leaves, but without the entire manuscript it was impossible to determine whether that text was accurate and complete. Houghton had by far the greatest collection of Keats's holographs; the bicentenary of his birth was just behind us, and we had mounted a handsome exhibition and held a lively symposium featuring scholars and writers from around the world. Surely the reintroduction of this important manuscript would represent a coup for the library and for Harvard.

There were problems, however; serious problems. The woman who owned this important fragment of the letter had possessed it for some time. Decades earlier, when she asked where her manuscript would find its most appropriate institutional home, she was told by everyone she consulted that it should go to Harvard. My great predecessor, Bill Jackson, arranged to meet her in Washington, but he so thoroughly offended her when they met that she not only decided to keep the manuscript, but also wrote scathing letters of denunciation to the president of the university and to the two sitting senators from the Commonwealth of Massachusetts. When I asked her on the telephone what it was that Jackson had said to her, she replied that Houghton's librarian insisted that her precious letter "belonged to Harvard."

Perhaps Jackson simply said (or intended to say) that the manuscript belonged *at* Harvard because the rest of the letter was already there, portions of it having been given to the university by Amy Lowell and Arthur Houghton. Our potential donor, on the other hand, had good reason to believe that the manuscript belonged to *her*, and she was un-

Self-Portrait With Donors

receptive to Jackson's manner, which she clearly thought was imperious. The fragment had been given to her by a friend, someone who knew that she would take good care of it after he died. She had waited decades before exploring, for a second time, how the manuscript might best be placed in a suitable library. When she consulted a group of new advisors, she received the same advice as before: it should really go to Cambridge. After exhausting all of the alternatives, she finally, reluctantly, had her friends set up another conversation with haughty Houghton.

The first question she asked me over the telephone was whether William Jackson was dead. I assured her that he was, that he had in fact died three decades earlier, in 1964. She did not know this, she said, and was relieved. Would I come to see her in Arizona? I explained that my parents lived just a few miles from her, in Scottsdale, and that I was planning to visit them for the Christmas holidays; it would give me great pleasure to see her then. She asked that we meet at her local bank in Phoenix. I told her that I would be wearing a navy blazer and a moustache. She responded that she would be wearing a navy sweat suit and looked like my grandmother. We had a date.

I was the first to arrive. An officer of the bank led me to a table in a secluded part of the lobby; over the loudspeaker system I could hear Elvis quietly singing "White Christmas." When my donor arrived at the table, I realized that she had already visited her safety-deposit box, for she had the framed fragment in her hands. She was very pleased to meet me, she said, but before giving me the manuscript she wanted to ask just a few more questions. "Are you sure that William Jackson is dead?" she asked. I assured her that this was the case. "Does Mr. Jackson's son work at the Houghton Library?" No, I assured her; he was a minister who taught at a theological seminary in Pittsburgh. This surprised her somewhat, but not as much as her next question surprised *me*. "There is a certain professor at Harvard," she said, "named Walter Jackson Bate, who has written a biography of Keats. Is he related to William Jackson?" No, I assured her. Jack was a good friend, and I could vouch for his upbringing in Indiana, far from Harvard and even further from Bill Jackson's native city of San Marino.

Finally, with a smile, she placed the manuscript in my hands — a difficult and brave gesture after more than thirty years of fretting over the unusual treasure her friend had given her. I agreed to have a suitable photocopy made that would fit right back into the frame. I told her about the exhibition in which the rest of her manuscript had enjoyed star billing; in return she took me back to her original encounter with my detested predecessor. "Mr. Jackson looked at the letter a long time," she said, "and then he read every word aloud, so I knew something was wrong. I am sure that he was tape-recording as he read, and that he was photographing it with a secret camera when he held the letter up to the light. And then he told me that it belonged to Harvard, and I knew that I couldn't trust him." Elvis was now singing "Silent Night." I told her that it was time to let bygones be bygones; her treasure was safe with me. I walked her to her car, wished her Merry Christmas, and then quietly walked over to my own car, carefully placing the framed manuscript on the seat next to me as I prepared to accompany John Keats on his rendezvous with destiny.

 Much of the work I did on behalf of the Houghton Library's collections and endowments involved similar expenditures of patience and persistence — and occasionally some ingenuity thrown in for good measure. It didn't begin that way, however. Three months after I arrived at the library, the much-loved curator of printing and graphic arts told me, very quietly, that she was thinking about retirement. Eleanor Garvey had worked at Harvard for almost her entire career and, in an environment that was often tumultuous, had always been able to keep her head above the fray. I would miss her dearly and I wanted to retire her in style. I consulted with my senior colleagues and we agreed upon what turned out to be an ambitious assortment of retirement gifts: a formal dinner, a research fund so that she could continue her work cataloguing her department's collection of Italian prints, a visiting fellowship in her honor, and the creation of a typeface ("Elli") that we could use on our invitations.

 I calculated that I needed a good $75,000 to pull this off (this was back in 1989, when $75,000 was a rather larger sum than it is today). I appealed first to Bill Bentinck-Smith, who volunteered his time for the university and who had been a close friend of Elli for many de-

Self-Portrait With Donors

> The Librarian of the Houghton Library
> requests the pleasure of your company
> for dinner at 17 Quincy Street, Cambridge
> on Friday, January nineteenth
> at six-thirty o'clock
>
> to honor Eleanor M. Garvey
> upon her retirement as
> the Philip Hofer Curator
> of Printing and Graphic Arts
>
> R s v p   Black tie
> 617·495·2441

cades. Bill kindly said that he wanted to make a significant contribution — but he also said that he would guarantee the entire sum if I had difficulty raising the rest. This was music to my ears, of course, and I have kept Bill's offer as a secret to this day, for it enabled me to approach other potential donors with some confidence and to tell my colleagues that they could immediately begin preparing those various forms of appreciation. How could they, they asked, if we didn't have the money in hand? "Don't worry," I said; "we'll find it." And sure enough Charlie Rheault came forward, as did another long-time friend of the library, Mel Seiden, who told me that raising that much money ought to be as difficult as falling off a boat. With the help of Houghton's closest friends, I didn't even have to disappear overboard.

But Harvard is a supertanker, not a small boat, and finding one's way to the captain's bridge was not an easy task. As the university entered the silent phase of its historic capital campaign in the 1990s, I had to jockey for position both within the College Library and within the central development office. I would suggest the names of potential donors and I would usually be turned down. Twice I was offered the opportunity to approach wealthy graduates whom I thought might support our initiatives, both times with the same phrase from my "handler" in Holyoke Center: "We haven't been able to get a dime out of him in ages. He's all yours." And neither did I, but at least I had the chance to try, and many of the friends of Houghton whom I also cultivated — always with the expert support of the curators — did come through, some of them in spectacular ways, including Florence Fearrington, who later endowed my position, and Julian Edison, who placed his family's name on the exhibition gallery.

But even as I was making progress on retiring Eleanor Garvey in style, I was also faced with a difficult situation, one that lasted for more years than I would like to remember. The first exhibition held at the library when I arrived was devoted to the 150th anniversary of photography, featuring the collection of Harrison D. Horblit, a Harvard graduate and omnivorous collector. The collection was on loan from his widow, Jean Horblit, who had promised that it would be given to Harvard. But the day after the grand opening of the exhibition, Jean asked to meet with me again and very sadly told me that she had decided not to donate the collection to Houghton; she was giving it, instead, to the Metropolitan Museum of Art. This was *not* music to my ears — let alone to the ears of those colleagues who had worked for years to keep this world-class collection firmly within Harvard's orbit. So Jean departed, accompanied (I later learned) by the curator of photography at the Met, who had made the trip to Cambridge with her.

All we could do, for the moment, was to keep in touch with Jean and let her know how much we valued her friendship. As time went by, we sent various trial balloons her way: we would pay for the cataloguing of the collection; we would pay to have a book stack in the library modified and customized to house the collection; we would create a campaign to endow a curatorship devoted to the collection.

Self-Portrait With Donors

All to no avail. Roger Stoddard and I twice drove down to see her in the house Harrison had purchased for them in rural Connecticut. It was so large that the furniture in the living room had to be custom-built so that its proportions would begin to resemble those of the room itself. It was so large that it was only on our second trip that I realized there was a stuffed polar bear standing in the foyer. But all to no avail, even when we dangled the possibility that the Fine Arts Department (in which I taught) and the Fogg Art Museum might join us in promoting photography at Harvard.

Finally, close to a state of genuine despair, I had a long talk with my colleague Joan Nordell, who had been "seconded" from the office of the University Librarian to Houghton for a year. You're going to have to do something completely different, she told me, and we therefore concocted an entirely new approach. Instead of telling Jean what Harvard was willing to do, I would instead tell her what *she* needed to do. We wouldn't take the collection, I wrote to her with a shaky hand, unless she pledged at least $2 million to catalogue it, house it, and endow a curatorship to take care of it. Two mornings later I received a call from her. "Now you're serious!" she said, and so we started mapping out just what each of us would do. What she needed, in other words, was a clear signal about how much the collection meant to us — and about how ambitious we would be on its behalf.

I share this episode with my graduate students in the arts management program at Bath Spa University each year, showing them that sometimes you can ask for too little as easily as too much. All of the procedures and techniques that my various development directors have shared with me have proved to be valuable, of course, and I know that I have profited a good deal from them: how to create a pyramid of major gifts for a campaign, how to set up a program of "moves management" (identifying potential donors, cultivating them, involving them, making an ask, stewarding them afterwards — and then asking them again, for if *you* don't, someone else will). But in my experience the crucial factor in successful development lies in the relationship that a director establishes with his or her donors. Fundraising, in my view, *should be another form of teaching*. My goal has always been to educate a potential donor about the institution's needs and aspirations, and to transfer the commitment and the passion *I* have for a specific project onto their shoulders as well.

In the best of all possible worlds, someone who makes a significant contribution will also serve as an ambassador among his or her own colleagues and friends. One of our supporters when I became the director of the Boston Athenæum, Joe Bain, had pledged a certain amount towards a planned-giving instrument. When he saw the various naming opportunities in our capital campaign, however, he decided that he should do much more, endowing the position of archivist in honor of his wife, Carol. In order to do so, he called upon a favor from a friend whose money he had been managing. That friend, Richard Diebold, made a contribution on behalf of the endowment and then agreed to see me when I was next in Arizona. We hit if off right away, for he, too, had been an academic — a very distinguished linguistic anthropologist — and had recently endowed a rather arcane professorship at Oxford so that it wouldn't disappear from the university's books. When the time came to raise funds for the Athenæum's 200th anniversary, I asked Richard he if would consider supporting our bicentennial exhibition and catalogue, both of which were promising to be quite expensive. A check for the full amount, almost half a million dollars, arrived just a few days later.

That's a success story twice over, but the disappointments are important and revealing as well. At Harvard we were approached by Leonard Bernstein's three children to see if we would be interested in taking on his immense archive. Of course we were interested, and the University Librarian, Sidney Verba, and the distinguished musicologist Christoph Wolff and I hosted a lunch for them in one of the rooms that Mary Hyde had created at the top of the library. The archive went, instead, to the Library of Congress. We vied for the archive of Pierre Matisse, the painter's grandson, who had been a successful gallery owner in New York. It went to the Morgan. We told Carter Burden, who had presented a hilarious talk at Houghton's fiftieth-anniversary symposium, that Harvard wanted his collection of American imprints — not just the high points, but those tens of thousands of titles that he had stored

Self-Portrait With Donors

in a warehouse. They went to the Morgan, too. And, as I have already mentioned, Sir Vidia Naipaul's archive went to Tulsa. But the Hyde Collection devoted to Samuel Johnson is very much now at home at the Houghton Library, and in that I take some pride along with a bestowal of belated thanks to Neil and Angelica Rudenstine, whose friendship with Mary was also crucial.

When I was first approached by the search firm that was charged with finding a new director for the Boston Athenæum, I immediately told them that they should be talking to one or two of my friends and colleagues instead of me. But "the two Nancies" did not give up very easily, and I eventually decided to have a conversation with the library's trustees. That meeting went well, and I realized that, if I were chosen, I would have a once-in-a-lifetime opportunity to mold the future of both the mission and the physical fabric of the institution. I also immediately sensed how eager the trustees were to support the new director in raising the funding to renovate and expand their landmark building. That was a pleasant surprise after years of having crimson-colored shackles placed on my wrists at Harvard. But there was another surprise in store for me as well. Before my appointment was announced in September 1996, I had a convivial lunch with the retiring director, Rodney Armstrong, another graduate of that small liberal-arts college in the Berkshires. We had known each other for several years, for Rodney had generously bestowed a membership on me while I was working at Harvard and living on Beacon Street just a few blocks from the Athenæum. As we talked about the eventual transition that would take place the following February, Rodney kindly informed me that he had included me in the plans he was making for his final Athenæum trip — to Como, Venice, and the Veneto — the following year.

Although I didn't let on to Rodney at the time, I was completely dumbfounded by what he had said. In all of my thinking about the Athenæum during the spring and summer of that year — in all of the planning I had done for the library's future — I had entirely forgotten that we sponsored annual trips abroad. As a member I did, of course, receive the brochures in the mail, but I simply associated these trips with another, later stage in my life when I would have the time and resources to enjoy them. The colorful itineraries would arrive; I would quickly look them over, sigh heavily as I saw how expensive the trip was, and then discard them. The trustees, moreover, had never mentioned these trips to me, presumably because Rodney had run the program entirely by himself, with the details to be worked out in far-away Philadelphia. I thought that I knew what I was getting into, but I had not counted on annual or semi-annual excursions to places like the Veneto.

But (Rodney continued) he had to share some unpleasant news with me as well. The cost of traveling in Europe was becoming much more dear. The hotels Athenæum travelers had traditionally favored were now often beyond our reach. He had reluctantly decided that we could no longer count on being able to stay at Grand hotels. Instead, he told me in subdued tones, we would have to settle for five-star hotels that were not always Grand. I still remember the disappointment in his eyes. And I still remember how completely surprised I was once again. Having lived in England as a graduate student for two years, having pursued most of my later research abroad on tiny academic stipends (they don't call them honoraria for nothing), I could remember staying at the "Ritz" in Lisbon, but it was a *pensão* directly across the street from the genuinely grand Ritz Hotel. You had a drink at the Connaught in London, but not a suite there. You looked out at the Russie in Rome, but you didn't stay there. You admired the architecture of the Crillon in Paris, but you didn't even dine there. I had traveled in Spain and in Greece on five dollars a day — and then ten. Five-star hotels would do quite nicely, I thought.

These excursions abroad, both for the Athenæum and now for the American Museum in Britain, have proven to be eye-opening in almost every possible way. I have learned a good deal about European history, and I think that I have also learned how to be an intelligent traveler: patient, forgiving, resigned to delays and cock-ups, watchful for unexpected opportunities. These trips are always pleasant, but they are also serious work, with a typical day of social interaction stretching from breakfast through an often late-night dinner. It's important that everyone be as comfortable as possible, and also crucial that those who travel on their own are invited to dinner on those wildly misnamed "free evenings." Just as important as the educational nature of these trips, moreover, is the opportunity to spend time with people who might wish to be involved in the future of your institution. Joe and Carol Bain were fellow travellers on my first Athenæum trip to England; another couple on that trip very generously underwrote an initiative to create a partnership devoted to civic discourse within Boston — a partnership that paired our patrician library with Suffolk University, which had for decades been a beacon of hope for members of the working class who aspired to a college education. And sometimes — no, probably most of the time — there are interesting surprises in addition to those generated by travelers who disappear in the middle of a visit to Meissen or who are caught walking the ramparts of an English country house hotel in their pajamas at midnight.

On a trip for Athenæum members to Rome, Amalfi, and Naples, for example, we had concocted a side-excursion to Gore Vidal's villa in Ravello, high above the Tyrrhenian Sea. The trip was a grueling one, for we spent much of the time outside, visiting ruins extending from Paestum to Pompeii, and the temperature was in the 90s every day. But even at the close of yet another eventful day, drinks with Gore Vidal and his partner Howard Austen seemed too good to miss. Besides, our extraordinary lecturer, Peter Lauritzen, knew Gore, and my former colleague and good friend from the Houghton Library, James Walsh, had built an extensive collection of Vidal's publications, including the mysteries he had written under the pseudonym of Edgar Box. James intended to bequeath his collection to Harvard, which we thought Gore might find pleasing, Gore having eschewed a Harvard education after graduating from Exeter and then again later, when he left the Navy. James, moreover, had signed up for this trip for the express purpose of meeting Gore for the first time.

It turned out to be a rather odd affair. We had difficulty, in the first place, finding the entrance to La Rondinaia. When we did, Howard warmly greeted us and took us in to meet our other host. Vidal was

James Walsh, Gore Vidal, Peter Lauritzen, and Richard Wendorf

already a legendary figure by this time, senatorial (if not quite an actual senator, like his grandfather), still filled with wit and charm as well as spleen. He turned out to be in good form, posing with us on a veranda that offered a breathtaking view of the coast and sea, and then sitting down with James and me in his office, whose walls were decorated with framed portraits of Gore from the covers of various magazines. He was disheveled, sporting a surprising number of food stains on his shirt, but engaging and more than a little focused on our ties with Harvard. He couldn't have cared less about the Boston Athenæum, as I quickly saw, but he was very keen to talk about the Houghton Library. James was, too, and so we passed a very pleasant hour together as Howard made sure that everyone had coffee, tea, or something stronger.

About a week after I returned to Boston, I received a call from an attorney in New York. He introduced himself as Andrew Auchincloss, the novelist Louis Auchincloss's son and Gore Vidal's lawyer. I told him that I had met his father at the Grolier Club in New York and that I had enjoyed meeting Gore in Ravello. How could I help? Well, he said, could I arrange for Gore's archive to go to the Houghton Library? I reminded him that I no longer worked for Harvard and that, as Gore had made clear during our time together, the first half of his archive had already gone to the University of Wisconsin. But I was not off the hook. Surely I could introduce him to the appropriate person at Harvard, and I assured him that I could: Leslie Morris, the curator of manuscripts, who had a good deal of experience working with living authors, including Harold Brodkey and John Updike. I gave Leslie a heads-up and thought no more of it.

A few weeks later I received another call from Gore's lawyer. Would Harvard be interested in owning Gore's villa, La Rondinaia? Gore and Howard were thinking of moving back to the United States, perhaps to Los Angeles again, and wanted to find the right owners for it. I reminded Counselor Auchincloss once again that I no longer worked for Harvard — and that the university already owned a rather wonderful estate outside of Florence, Bernard Berenson's Villa I Tatti. And once again I put him in touch with the right person at

Harvard and thought no more about it. But the wheels were in motion. Wisconsin agreed to a transfer of materials, the other half of the archive made its way to Houghton, James's bequest entered the collection — and Harvard wisely decided that La Rondinaia was probably one Italian villa too many.

So there you have it: one thing can lead to another until the cultural landscape has shifted again just a little. And I think it's rather marvelous that Gore is now ensconced in the Houghton Library, and that he has left his entire estate, including future royalties from his work, to Harvard, possibly worth more than $35 million — much to the surprise of his friends and the dismay of his relatives. One can be captious about the quality of his endeavors in each of the three genres in which he wrote — fiction, plays, essays and memoirs — and there may be a shred of truth in Michael Lind's comment that Vidal was a middlebrow's idea of a highbrow. But I can think of few authors who were so well placed within the world of American letters during his lifetime. Gore seemed to know everyone, and he corresponded with most of them. He aspired to be the liberal, enlightened conscience of what he mischievously referred to as the United States of Amnesia. Like John Cheever before him, he finally made it to Harvard, and he did so on his own terms.

CHAPTER NINE

Libraries, Museums — and Me

Soon after I arrived at the Boston Athenæum in 1997, a few of my new colleagues and trustees took me aside and asked me whether we were a library, a museum, or a cultural center. What was — or ought to be — our essential mission? These were questions not entirely dissimilar to many I had fielded at Harvard. Why did Houghton put on so many exhibitions? Did it need both a lecture series and a program of chamber music every year? Why, I was asked to explain to several College Librarians (to whom I reported), was Houghton buying and exhibiting artists' books? Shouldn't they go into the Fine Arts Library? Why had I created a fellowship program for visiting scholars? Weren't we supposed to be supporting Harvard's own faculty and students? As part of our strategic planning process at the American Museum, we have been asking ourselves similar questions concerning scope and definition. Is our focus squarely on decorative and folk art, or do we have a broader mission to educate the public about the wider sweep of American history and culture? Should the museum respect our founders' decision to limit the accumulation of objects to the period between 1690 and 1860, as Winterthur had done, or should we take the leap into the twentieth (and twenty-first) centuries? And what do we make of the fact that we have a manor house and an exhibition gallery surrounded by 125 acres of land and some of the most beautiful views in the southwest of England? Are we an American museum (with gardens) or should we aspire to be the American Museum *and* Gardens?

Part of the role of a library or museum director is to stimulate this kind of discussion if it doesn't already exist. Opinions should be heard and a new consensus should be reached. Institutional history — and tradition — should be consulted, but they should not be allowed to restrict the development of what is essentially an organic entity. In the case of the Boston Athenæum, that history was entirely relevant, for the institution had originated as a library in 1807 and then, within two decades, had become the city's most important site for the exhibition of paintings and sculpture. Once the trustees had assisted in creating the Museum of Fine Arts in the Back Bay in the 1870s — with a significant transfer of artwork on long-term loan — the Athenæum became primarily a library again, so much so that a new generation of trustees, early in the twentieth century, worked hard to reinvigorate the art collection, a process that is still in place today.

And so I told my questioners back in 1997 that the institution was a cultural hybrid: yes, it was primarily a research and lending library, but it had a strong art collection and exhibition program, and it served as a cultural center not just for its members but increasingly for the general public as well. *And it was entirely fine for the institution to have such a multiple identity.* (Just think of the Huntington with its library, art galleries, and gardens.) To narrow the Athenæum's focus — to see it only as a large working library — would be tantamount to clipping its wings as an institution. The Athenæum is not unique (I immediately think of the Redwood Library in Newport), but it is a rare example of how an early nineteenth-century institution can remain vibrant and relevant more than two hundred years later. Stewart Brand has taught us "how buildings learn." We have to listen carefully to hear how the institutions housed within those buildings can continue to learn as well.

Libraries and museums are different from each other in several important ways, of course, and they may do their "learning" differently as well. Both the Houghton Library and the Boston Athenæum mount exhibitions based on their own collections or on materials that have been loaned to them, but they don't charge admission for their exhibitions and the number of visitors they attract is therefore not a critical issue. The Houghton Library is partly funded by Harvard University (through the College Library) and even more so through income from its many endowments. The Boston Athenæum relies on its large endowment as well, but it is also sustained through its membership and a particularly successful annual appeal. The American Museum, on the other hand, like most independent museums and galleries in the United States and the United Kingdom, relies heavily on the revenue it generates through admission tickets, its retail program, and its café. Membership plays a part, as do increasingly resilient annual appeals in both countries, but the importance of a successful annual exhibition exerts a good deal of influence on how those exhibitions are chosen and how they are then marketed.

For the museum's fiftieth anniversary in 2011, for example, I was able to convince the collector David Gainsborough Roberts to lend us his collection of Marilyn Monroe's dresses and personalia. This was frowned upon, at first, by some of the museum's long-time supporters, but the exhibition was so successful — and the revenue earned was so high — that it is now considered the kind of show that we should aspire to offer each year. Even national museums in Britain, such as the V&A, Tate, and Liverpool, need to maintain high levels of visitation in order to justify the central government's support. These museums are not allowed to charge for general admission, but they do charge for admission to their special exhibitions — and thus the need for those blockbuster shows for which London in particular has become so well known.

I'm not suggesting that the work of a library director is necessarily easier than that of a museum director. If you've read my earlier chapter on the Houghton Library, you have some sense of the different kinds of problems and pressures that are brought to bear on academic libraries as well as independent ones. Nor am I suggesting that the life of a director of a national museum in Britain is relatively easy: working with the central government is a continual struggle, and the need for additional revenue is always a daunting reality. But independent museums, unless they enjoy significant endowments, will always be stretched to adapt their "offer" to a constantly changing audience.

What libraries and museums do enjoy in common is their status as special cultural entities within the larger social and commercial worlds in which we live. Let me share a story that my friend (and fellow director) Steven Parissien and I enjoy telling on each other. About two years ago I visited Steven at Compton Verney, a lovely museum in Warwickshire, in order to see the exhibition of English landscapes he had curated based on works that are normally stored away in the basement of Tate Britain. It was an impressive show, and as we wandered from painting to painting and room to room we became quite animated, with Steven becoming especially excited about one of the pictures he had been able to include. At that point we were approached by a gentleman who had broken away from a docent tour across the gallery. Looking rather fiercely at both of us, he said, "Don't you realize that this is a museum? You're making so much noise that we can't hear what our docent is saying!"

We bit our tongues and gave each other rather bemused looks, and as I continued to think about this exchange (well, not quite an *exchange*: we simply clammed up) as I made my way back to my own museum, I had a number of conflicting thoughts. The first, of course, was an appreciation of the irony of the situation, in which two museum directors had to be reminded of where they were standing. The second was that it was terrific that these museum-goers were hanging on the docent's every word: that spoke volumes, so to speak, on behalf of all of them. The third was a sense of mild embarrassment that we had become so animated that we were actually distracting other visitors. But my final response (the one I wish to examine here) was to think more generally about the kinds of behavior we would like to see displayed by the thousands of people who visit our museums each year. What's wrong with two people talking excitedly about a particular painting? Don't we, more than anything, want our visitors to become engaged with what they are viewing, and isn't a vigorous conversation just what the arts should generate? Why should galleries become hushed temples of visual culture? Isn't there room for a museum of exuberance, both in the art that is displayed there and in our reaction to it?

And now the inevitable caveats. No, I'm not condoning the kind of behavior that is so intrusive that it prevents other visitors from concentrating on the art that is on display. We've all had exasperating experiences of this kind, often in our larger museums, where surging crowds focus on a particular iconic object, cameras in hand and phones at the ready. The Louvre has been forced to place *Mona Lisa* in a large room of its own, which does nothing but increase the volume of the audience and produce an even more claustrophobic at-

Libraries, Museums — and Me

mosphere. The Sistine Chapel suffers the same perils no matter how often the guards shout out their futile "silenzios!" And the telephones and cameras producing "selfies" in which visitors mimic the poses in back of them have created a new phenomenon that obviously cuts both ways: some may think of it as an act of engagement while others will judge it to be both disrespectful and an impediment to the next viewer's engagement with the object at hand.

I don't wish to adjudicate these dilemmas. I do wonder, however, just how galleries devoted to painting, sculpture, prints, and drawings became the hushed, hallowed sepulchers they often appear to be — or aspire to be. Like several other writers, I've argued that libraries, museums, and concert halls have become the chapels and cathedrals of an increasingly secularized society. Libraries and concert halls naturally call for a respectful silence as readers and listeners engage with texts and performances. But is a hushed atmosphere the healthiest way in which to engage with visual art? And isn't an exchange between two (or among several) viewers one of the social and cultural productions that artists hope to generate?

I served as a trustee of Boston's Museum of Fine Arts for a decade before moving to England, and nothing gave me more pleasure than taking my children, when they were still fairly young, through a few galleries on Saturday mornings. I always gave them the same assignment: after half an hour or so, tell me which one painting you would like to take home with us, and why. They enjoyed this exercise and they excelled at it, blending emotional responses with increasingly solid aesthetic ones. And they both became excited, just as Steven and I had done, and inevitably they provoked a raised Bostonian eyebrow or two. I thought that was just fine then — and I still do today. Nothing gives me more satisfaction at my own museum than hearing animated conversation and laughter well up within the central hallway of the manor house. I sometimes take a look down at our visitors from my perch on the top floor — and then I return to my office and shut the door, judging the hubbub below to be at least one sign that we are doing a decent job.

Libraries are *not* institutions of exuberance, at least not outwardly so, but they do share a museum's commitment to aesthetic and intellectual stimulation and exchange, and they also share the continuing need for enlightened support. The nature of that support, even from private individuals and foundations, began to change during the past two decades. Potential donors are no longer solely the offspring of established families with ample resources and traditional cultural commitments. They are now just as likely to be — and in many cities *more* likely to be — successful figures within the financial and commercial sectors. And because these new generations of donors are steeped in the world of investments and competing markets, they are more likely to wish to ensure that the contributions they make are good investments as well. They are more sharply focused on an institution's finances, on its levels of giving (especially among trustees), on the costs of new programs and on the outcomes that can be predicted. They want, in other words, for their gifts to be part of a viable business plan, and they are more likely than their predecessors to offer advice and to monitor a library or museum's progress. This is sometimes called "philanthrocapitalism," and it has led not just to expressions of gratitude but also to concerns — even suspicions — about the intentions of many wealthy donors.

I began to sense this shift in the pattern of giving when I worked in Boston, and I have heard a good deal about it from friends who run organizations in other American cities, particularly in New York. But this is not yet the state of affairs in Britain, which has a philanthropic environment that is not nearly as mature — or as generous — as in America. There are deeply historical reasons for this, primarily the central government's role as the sole source of revenue for libraries and museums during most of the twentieth century. This was never quite a genuinely socialist nation, but it *is* a nation that still expects its government to provide the resources for its health care, its universities, and its cultural institutions. This state of affairs is slowly changing, driven by cutbacks in government funding and, as a consequence, the need for private giving. But because there has never been a culture of philanthropy in Britain — and because the current tax laws do not reward individual giving as generously as they do in the United States — this is not yet

Libraries, Museums — and Me

a fully viable development. Individuals in Britain are often generous in a modest way, but most of the private funding that makes its way into the cultural realm comes from trusts and foundations established by successful entrepreneurs. A few institutions, including the American Museum, have the ability to raise funds within the United States as well, and if it were not for our American supporters, my museum would not be able to undertake the ambitious plans it now has for new period rooms (Frank Lloyd Wright, "California modern"), nor for the expansion of its American gardens.

In spite of their dissimilarities, the three institutions for which I have had the privilege of providing direction possess two significant elements in common. In the first place — and completely by happenstance — all three have celebrated important anniversaries during my tenure. When I arrived at the Houghton Library in 1989, I soon realized that our fiftieth anniversary was on the horizon, in 1992, and that no planning had begun, presumably because the staff was waiting for the arrival of its new director. Much needed to be accomplished as quickly as possible, and that included finding the funding to support what turned out to be a fairly ambitious program. But once we had the backing of some generous friends, everything fell nicely into place: we mounted major exhibitions, published handsome catalogues, held formal dinners as well as events designed to bring a wider cross-section of the university community into the library and, as I have already mentioned, we concluded our year by hosting an international symposium on the future of special collections libraries. I edited the proceedings of the symposium, and the University Library and Harvard University Press made sure that it had appropriate currency both within and beyond the precincts of Harvard Yard.

When I arrived at the Boston Athenæum in 1997, the institution's 200th anniversary was, as I noted with some relief, ten years in the future. That interval quickly began to shrink, however, as we engaged in the task of raising almost $30 million and then began the three-year renovation and expansion of our building, opening it anew in 2002. Believing that the combination of elements at Harvard would also work well at the Athenæum, I set an agenda for 2007 that included an exhibition devoted to our collections which became so ambitious that it occupied not just our new gallery but most of the real estate on the ground floor of the library as well. The exhibition catalogue, *Acquired Tastes*, was just as voluminous, and it was accompanied by a volume I edited on the history of membership libraries in America and, slightly later, a volume devoted to the first two hundred years of the Athenæum's history. And we concluded our celebrations by asking colleagues from around the country to tell us — trustees, staff members, and our general membership — what the future of reading, publishing, and libraries would be like.

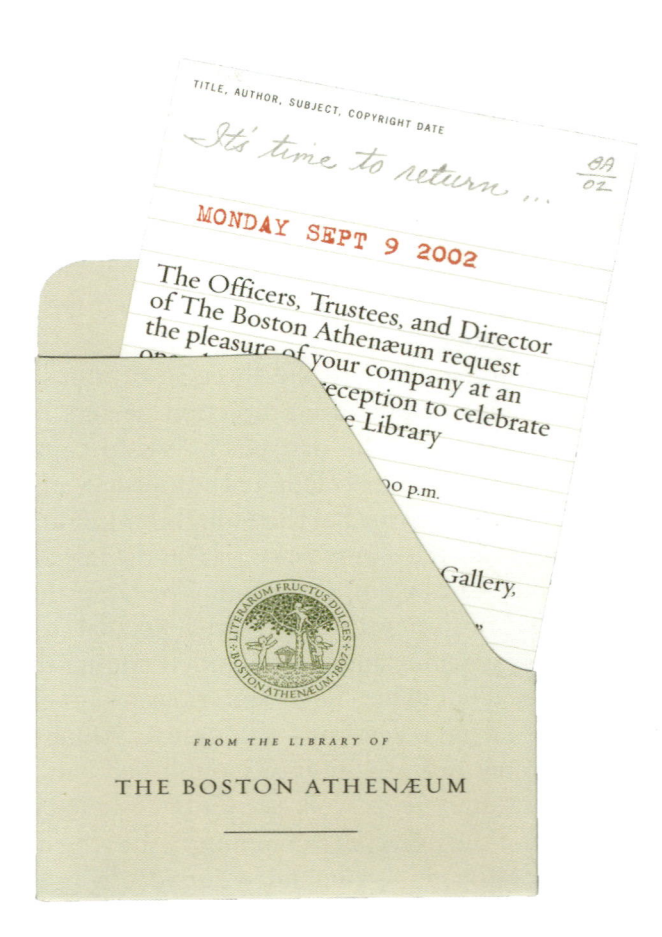

Libraries, Museums — and Me

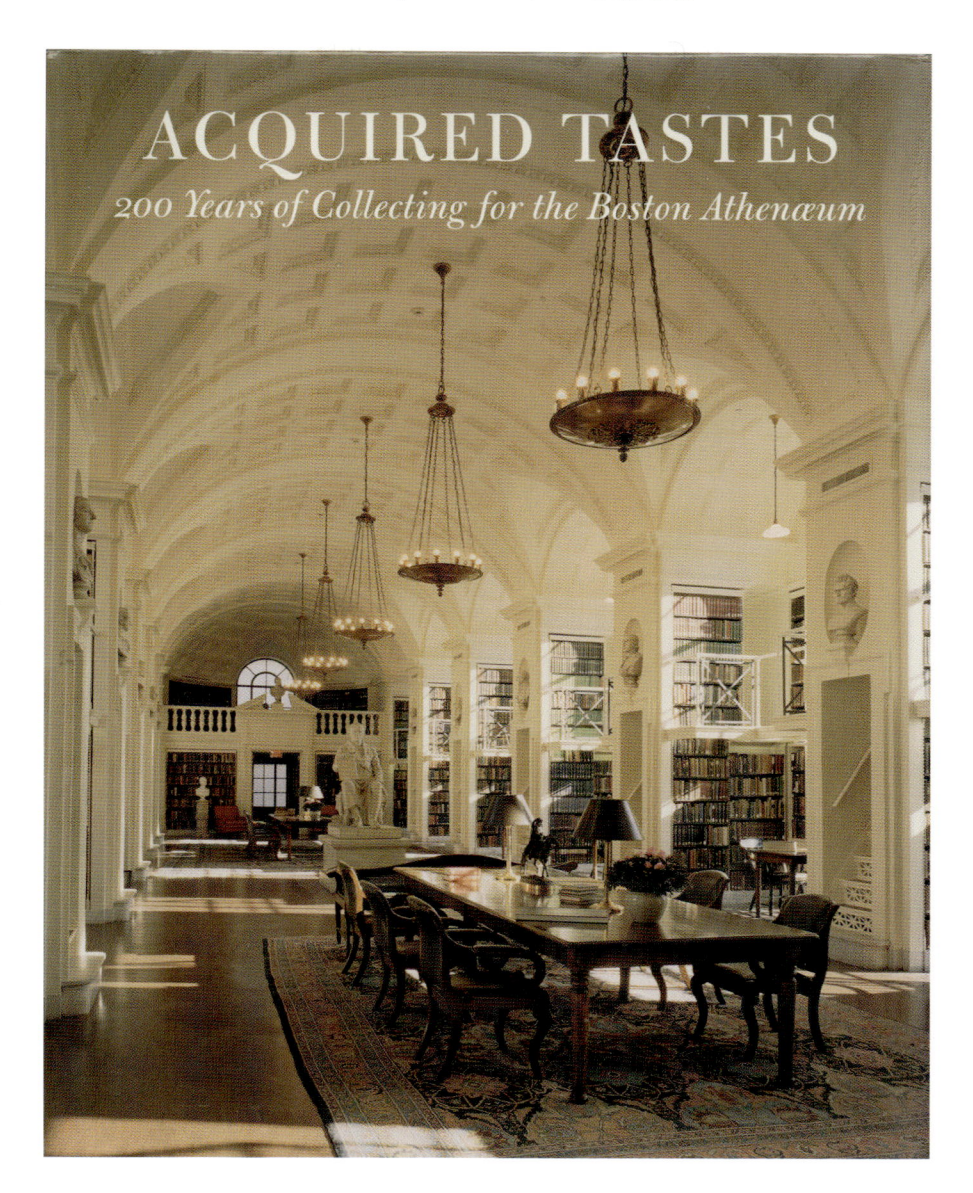

ACQUIRED TASTES
200 Years of Collecting for the Boston Athenæum

RICHARD WENDORF

AMERICA'S
MEMBERSHIP
LIBRARIES

Edited by Richard Wendorf

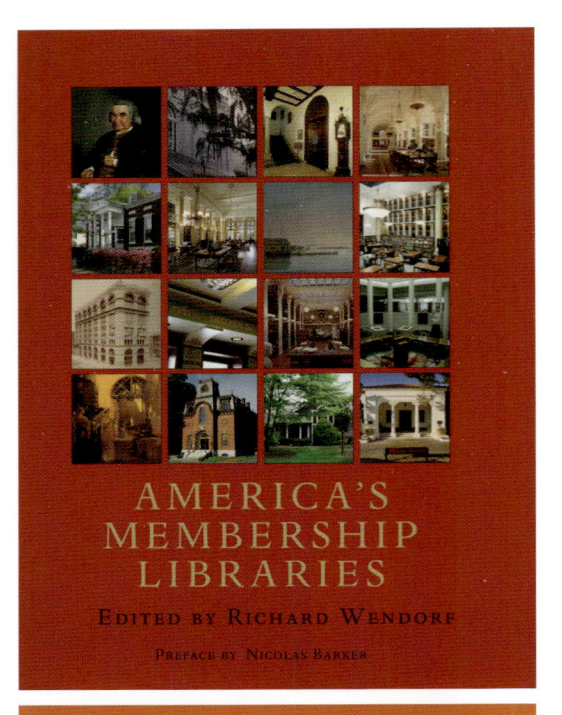

Preface by Nicolas Barker

THE BOSTON ATHENÆUM

Bicentennial
Essays

Edited by
Richard Wendorf

Libraries, Museums — and Me

When I accepted the trustees' offer to become the director of the American Museum in Britain in 2010, I therefore did so with my eyes wide open, for the museum's fiftieth anniversary loomed precariously close, just one year away, and I actually wrote a plan for the trustees before I moved to England and received my first pay check. The trustees and staff had already committed themselves to the renovation of the estate's coach house and stables (to become seminars rooms and an auditorium space) and to the reinstallation of the important folk art collection in a gallery that had previously served as the manor house's billiard room and as the museum's café. In addition to these capital projects, we mounted an exhibition of the museum's treasures in the manor house and the "Marilyn — Hollywood Icon" show in the exhibition gallery. We published catalogues for both exhibitions, held a pop-up show at Christie's in London, issued a catalogue of the map collection, and fêted the great and the good, including Winston Churchill's only surviving child, at an anniversary luncheon on the museum's lawn, with commemorative medals presented to the particularly important (and generous) great and good. I should add, moreover, that the two exhibitions, the three publications, and the three newly renovated spaces were all opened or published on the same day, a schedule that I would not recommend to anyone in the library or museum world.

I have therefore become, entirely by accident, a connoisseur of institutional anniversaries, and in the process I have become more and more convinced that it is just as important to look forward as it is to glance backward on such occasions. The symposia at Houghton and the Boston Athenæum attempted to do just that, and in all three cases the conclusion of the anniversary year also marked the beginning of strategic planning. The experience of "forward" planning, as we call it in Britain, can be frustrating and even difficult. Staff members and trustees may well not see eye to eye. Some members of the staff who have felt neglected in the past can become strident in their efforts to have their voices heard. The high hopes and expectations of staff members may not match the realities of future funding. Facilitators can be surprisingly effective or surprisingly tone-deaf; I was fortunate to work with one in Cambridge and Boston who had perfect pitch. In the case of the American Museum, it was important to hold discussions not just in Bath and in London, but in New York as well — and then, as director, to synthesize the various conversations and send out drafts for further consultation. But despite the various obstacles and pitfalls that may well plague a strategic planning process, I cannot think of a more important joint enterprise for an institution once the parties and exhibitions are behind you and the stark reality of the future is staring you in the face. (The American Museum's house, Claverton Manor, will celebrate its 200th anniversary in 2020. Perhaps the Jane Austen Society will come to my rescue.)

The second important element these three institutions share is their relatively modest and manageable scale. Houghton is one of the world's largest and most important repositories of rare books and manuscripts, but it is not the Harvard College or Harvard University Library; it is simply part of it. The Boston Athenæum is by far the largest membership library in America and is overshadowed by the

Libraries, Museums — and Me

London Library only by the number of books on its shelves; but it is not nearly as large as a national library nor an encyclopedic museum. The American Museum is the largest institution of its kind in the southwest of England, but it is run on a relatively modest budget, by a small and talented staff, and with the support of a large number of dedicated volunteers. It would, in fact, be difficult to overestimate the importance of these volunteers, who serve as room guides and tour guides and assist us with special events and with improvements in the gardens. Our cohort of almost 150 close friends is essential to the operation of a museum of our size and is certainly out of scale with the needs of most libraries.

This question of scale has been (and remains) important to me for two reasons. It is possible to manage such a library or museum, in the first place, without losing a sense of how each facet of the institution actually works — and performs. With the exception of the cataloguing of rare books, manuscripts, and works of art (which I leave to the experts on my staff), it has been possible for me to become involved in a wide range of institutional issues in either a hands-on or hands-mostly-off manner, depending on the situation. At the American Museum, for instance, I take joint responsibility for the exhibitions we mount, the gardens we design (and re-design), decisions about membership and admissions, our lectures and concerts, the development program, and even the dishes we offer in our café. I assist in determining and designing our trips for supporters, and I chose the font — Galliard, that handsome Anglo-American typeface created by Matthew Carter — through which we present ourselves to the world. There are professional satisfactions in such an environment that I have been very reluctant to relinquish.

And then there is the other side of the coin, the more personal one. When I made the decision to leave my professorial career at Northwestern and to become a full-time administrator at Harvard, I did so with the understanding that I would continue to teach and that I would keep my life as a practicing scholar alive. That has not always been easy, especially when my children were young and there were other demands upon my time. The decision to move from one institution to another, which I have now done three times, also disrupts progress on one's scholarly work, as does the occasional move from one home to another, which I have done ten times (yes, ten times) since moving to Boston and thence to England. But opportunities for teaching and a continuing commitment to research and writing have provided the backbone, the central core, of a professional career that has taken several swings and roundabouts, as the English like to say. This is partly a matter of personal fulfillment; it is partly a deeply ingrained habit; but it is also partly a way of making a distinction between my institutional life and my more personal one. When my children were young, we were walking down Boston's Charles Street one weekend when one of my acquaintances greeted me by saying "Good morning, Mr. Athenæum!" Who was she, they asked? The sister of one president, I replied, and the aunt of the current one. Their eyes widened for a moment and then they began to tease me about my newly coined name. And that was fine, just as it is when I am (more likely than not) introduced to someone in Bath or London as the director of the American Museum. It has always felt good to be the face of a cultural institution, but it is also important to have a name, a face, a life of one's own. And having your own name on the title-page of a book or at the beginning of an article is, for me, the most deeply satisfying way to do so. As Flaubert said, "Let us intoxicate ourselves with ink, since we lack the nectar of the gods."

Scholarship and writing — and books increasingly designed for a broader audience — have therefore remained the backbone of my career as a library and museum director. I've always had a fairly good sense of which writing project will come next even if my progress within those books and essays hasn't always been that clear. Meandering remains something of a virtue, I believe: it has shaped my interests as a collector as well as a scholar, and it is one way (at least) to describe my path from one institution to another. That professional trajectory can also be characterized by a gradual abandonment of institutional safety nets. I'm not sure whether I am the last university professor in the United States to forsake a tenured position in order to become a library or museum director, but I am certainly one of the

Libraries, Museums — and Me

very last to do so. Serving as the librarian of the Houghton Library placed me in a position almost as secure as a tenured professorship — but the difference between the security offered by those two roles was nevertheless a palpable one. The next step was natural but even more precarious as I reported to an ever-changing board of trustees; and my final move, to the directorship of a museum — a museum in another country, moreover, with two boards of trustees serving on two continents — has exposed me to further vicissitudes, as I have already recounted. The only safety net I now enjoy is one based on the performance of the institution and on our blueprints for the future, and I wouldn't be entirely honest if I didn't say that there are times (not many, but a few) when the memory of having secured a tenured professorship over half a lifetime ago offers little comfort indeed.

CHAPTER TEN

Highly Skilled Migrant

In June 2016 I marched over to the Guildhall in the center of Georgian Bath, affirmed my allegiance to crown and country, became a dual citizen, and thereby relinquished my peculiar status as a "highly skilled migrant" in the eyes of the Home Office. The entire process takes more than six years. It is tiresome, frustrating, and expensive — but rather easier than qualifying for a British driver's license. High time, I thought, to take stock of my experience in my adopted home and to reflect on the ways in which Britain has changed (and, in some ways, has stayed the same) since I first lived here more than forty years ago.

I thought that the transition would be fairly smooth. I had, after all, visited London almost every year since I took my degree at Oxford. I knew the libraries and museums reasonably well, and I had enjoyed living for part of seven consecutive summers in a charming mews house in South Kensington. I had visited Bath as a student and then, just before I made my move, I delivered a lecture at the Bath Royal Literary and Scientific Institution, where I now serve as a trustee. What I did not realize, however, was the extent to which so much of what you need to know about living in England is surprisingly difficult to ascertain. Whoever said that Britain and America were two countries divided by a common language — and it seems to have been Oscar Wilde — might have said the same about the conventions of daily life, which appear to be similar but are often quite different.

This country quite famously has an "unwritten constitution" — there is no central document to consult such as America's Constitution and Bill of Rights — and this places great weight on a variety of acts, statutes, and precedents in common law. I suppose the same could be said of how you make sense of the nation's scattered rules and regulations as they affect your personal life. No one told me that I needed to have a National Insurance Number, or register for the National Health Service, or choose a medical practice (rather unhappily called a "surgery") in Bath. No one told me that you could procure a senior rail card at age 60 or a senior bus card that allows you to travel free of charge throughout the country. No one told me that my American driver's license was only valid for one year in England, after which I would have to obtain a British one. I learned this from my insurance company, which refused to cover me when I attempted to renew. Had the company told me beforehand, I could have qualified for a second license while my American one was still valid; instead, I spent five months not being able to drive my car while I waited and waited to take the tests that would finally put me back on the road. No one told me that a shuttle bus from the Museum picked up colleagues each morning directly across from where I first lived ("We thought you knew but preferred taxis"). And even more importantly, no one told me that you cannot transfer funds from the US into the UK without severe tax consequences. (You essentially lose your seven-year benefit of not being taxed on what is rather grandly called your "global income.")

Before I made my move, I printed out a voluminous guide for Americans moving to the UK. Not one of these points was covered. Even during the six-and-a-half-year immigration process, there is no summary that tells you that once you qualify for "indefinite leave to remain" you have to wait another year before applying for citizenship. (Leave to remain: one of the most confusing labels I've come across so far and almost as amusing as "garden leave" or "time in lieu.") Nor are you informed that citizenship merely qualifies you to apply for a passport and that you are *de facto* "grounded" in Britain until that passport comes through (because you have to relinquish your residency card when you become a citizen, and you have to send your American passport to the Home Office in order to receive a British one). You also have to appear for an interview in order to receive a passport even though an interview is not required for either "indefinite leave" or citizenship. Go figure.

And so I have stumbled about much of the time, catching information on the fly, listening closely to the advice of friends, reading *The Times* each morning and watching the BBC news in the evening. Much of what I have learned about the practicalities of English life has been gleaned from conversations with fellow inhabitants of the men's locker room at the Bath Spa Hotel, where I work out or swim in the morning. My friends there have found me a physician, a house cleaner, a trustee for the museum, and even a glamorous apartment (as I relate in the following chapter). I have learned what *not* to say in terms of verbal etiquette: toilet (loo, please), pardon (excuse me), lounge (sitting room), living room (sitting room), couch (sofa), scotch (whisky), hors d'oeuvres (canapés), or dessert (pudding). I have made a list of Britishisms that runs several pages in length, all of whose entries are *not* included in a very useful 400-page book entitled *British English A to Zed*.

I have also learned that it is no longer proper to arrive at a dinner on time; one should be five to ten minutes late. Canapés must be on the light side, usually a bowl of nuts and a dish of cheesy biscuits. Champagne is the preferred cocktail, although prosecco is often offered as a substitute, and a gin and tonic can still be served without reproach. I have a butler's tray in my sitting room that is heavily stocked with spirits and cordials, thanks to gifts from visitors and thank-yous when I deliver the odd graduation address. I have rarely had an English friend ask to sample any of its delights, whereas my American friends can't wait to drink the whisky, vodka, and brandy. This is still a country of serious drinkers, but I have only once been asked by a guest for a glass of beer. Wine follows the champagne, usually French whites and reds, and occasionally port to go with pudding or cheese if the evening turns out to be a "jolly" one. Granted, I don't hang out in bars and pubs, but I think it's safe to say that a "proper" dinner in London or one of the outlying cities — Oxford, Cambridge, Winchester, Bath — would play itself out pretty much as I have described it.

It's been said that the British still excel at four things: soldiering, tailoring, character acting, and vomiting in public. Let me address this last charge first. When I was a graduate student at Princeton, my friends were especially fond of telling the following joke.

> An Englishman and his wife arrive in Paris, where his wife suddenly dies. He decides to buy a black hat suitable for mourning wear and enters a nearby de-

partment store. His French is rather shaky, however, and instead of asking for a '*chapeau noir*' he asks for a '*capottes*,' which is French slang for a condom. '*Avez-vous des capottes noirs?*' he inquires. The clerk asks him why it must be black. '*Parce que ma femme, ma femme est mort.*' To which the clerk replies, '*quelle délicatesse!*'

There are many versions of this story, some stipulating an American couple, some substituting an overcoat (*capotte anglais*) for a hat. It was included, I later discovered, in G. Legman's classic *Rationale of the Dirty Joke*, but this would have been of little interest to those of us who were budding literary scholars rather than cultural anthropologists. All we had to do was repeat *quelle délicatesse* in an appropriate context, at precisely the right moment, in order to bring the house down. It worked every time.

Quelle politesse: this used to be a country not just of delicacy of feeling but also of polite behavior. If anything, the English in particular were known, in years gone by, as exceptionally polite people. When badgered by detective inspectors in Joseph Losey's *Blind Date* (1959), for instance, the Dutch painter played by Hardy Krüger tells his inquisitors that he "thought the English were supposed to be polite." This is a much less polite society than the one I knew in the 1970s, and the rudeness is now endemic, not just the effect of the country attracting and absorbing millions of tourists and immigrants. Young and middle-aged Britons in particular have become louder, ruder, and more aggressive than their parents and grandparents. Many seem to take pleasure in "jumping the queue," or deliberately stepping behind your car while you are backing into a parking space, or forcing you off the sidewalk (the pavement, that is) as they walk two or three abreast. When well-dressed men and women allow a door to slam in my face — and then superficially apologize — I tell them not to worry, that I've lived in England for over five years and that I've gotten used to the rudeness. And what I observe on the pavement I sense even more strongly when I drive my car about town. For all of the regulation that has been imposed on modern society here — especially in the abundance of traffic signs and bizarrely painted roads — Britain still seems to have spawned generations of horn-heavy drivers who have made a competitive sport of getting from A to B before you do.

But the public drinking, the behavior at sporting events, and the expanded girth of John Bull are not unique to the British Isles; these are ubiquitous social factors across the continent — and not least in America. What is unusual is the rapidity — and the comprehensiveness — with which these changes have taken place. Gone are the days in which you would be greeted in a shop by someone asking "May I help you?" or even (as in the title of the much-loved television series) "Are you being served?" Most of the time the younger workers ask, with or without looking directly at you, "You all right?" And when you thank them, they simply reply "No problem." Or even worse, "No problem, mate." As one of my friends sometimes fumes, "I am *not* your mate!" But perhaps we are all mates together these days; even David Cameron urged us to "hug a hoodie." And when I survey the audience at a performance in Bath or London — even at the opera houses — I am taken aback by the number of people who arrive in jeans and t-shirts. Yes, there will always (we are assured) be opera at Glyndebourne with dinner jackets and pearls, but there is often a vast wasteland between formal wear and blue jeans.

This rudeness can permeate professional life as well. At the bidding of one of the American Museum's supporters, I agreed to have a breakfast meeting with a young man who was interested in having his agency create public events for us. We agreed to meet at a well-known restaurant in London at 8:30; I had it in my diary. Because I wanted to make sure that I arrived on time, I took a taxi and expected to arrive a few minutes early. But at 8:25 I received a call asking me where I was. The meeting was set for 8 o'clock, he told me, and he had left the restaurant to go to work. I said that we had agreed on 8:30 and that I was almost there. When I entered the restaurant, I mentioned to the maître-d' that I was meeting this young man, who had already arrived and left. Oh no, I was told; my host had not shown up yet. He didn't arrive until almost 9, which gave me some time to consider how to handle someone who was not only deceitful, but who had also

Highly Skilled Migrant

attempted to make me feel off-balance and defensive. I had three options, I thought, somewhat relishing the dramatic irony at play here. I could simply leave and send him a withering email. I could confront him when he arrived. Or I could have breakfast with him and see whether he would apologize for his behavior. In all three scenarios, his firm would certainly not be getting the museum's business. You will not be surprised to learn that I decided to choose the third option, not least because I wanted to see first-hand just how he would behave. And of course he never apologized — nor did he realize that it was I who actually had the upper hand.

This odd incident was made all the more telling to me because of a story I had heard a year earlier from a London taxi driver. I was on the phone with my personal assistant, telling her that the arrangements had been made for my presenting a talk on portraiture in a few weeks' time. The cabbie listened to the conversation and then congratulated me on taking an interest in portraiture: that, he said, was "proper painting," not the kind of thing being created today by the likes of Tracey Emin. It turned out that Tracey Emin had been in his cab two or three times, each time using certain Anglo-Saxon nouns that he could not in all decency repeat. "I can't bring myself to tell you what they were, sir, but the worst began with the third letter of the alphabet." He then asked me if I knew a well-known gallery owner in Mayfair. I said that I knew who he was, but that I didn't know him personally. At which point the cabbie told me the following story. Two years ago he was driving in Mayfair when a large Jaguar drove into the side of his taxi, doing a good deal of damage to one of the cab's "wings." The cabbie exchanged insurance information with the other driver, paid to have the damage repaired, and waited for a long time — over a year, I believe — to have the driver's company reimburse him. This was a financial burden for the cabbie, who implored both the gallery owner and the insurance company to pay him. "He's got paintings worth millions of pounds hanging on his walls. Why couldn't he make me good?"

Half a year after the reimbursement finally came through, he saw the gallery owner on the pavement with two suitcases in hand. He pulled over, placed the luggage in the front of his cab, and headed out to Heathrow. When he reached the final stretch of highway, he pulled onto the grass and asked the gallery owner whether he recognized him. He didn't, so the cabbie reminded him of how he had been treated, placed the two suitcases on the grass beside the taxi, and told his passenger to get out of the cab. The gallery owner refused, arguing that he would miss his flight. The cabbie then said, "You have greatly inconvenienced me, and now I'm going to inconvenience you. Either you leave the cab now or I will pull you out." The gallery owner left the cab, very unhappily, and the cabbie then received a visit from two police constables a few days later. He told them the entire story, at the end of which the two officers laughed, clapped him on the back, and left him in peace.

Accurate, embellished, or apocryphal as this story may be — and I rather think that it is true, given the context in which it was imparted to me — it draws a clear distinction between the behavior of one generation of Englishmen and that of a younger one. The older chap, our spunky cabbie, finally had the last laugh, even if he did so at some cost. It struck me later that Tracey Emin had gotten off rather lightly.

These divisions between and among the generations provide one way in which to map the social and cultural factors now at play within British society. When I was a student at Oxford, I thought that the most significant social marker was whether one had taken a university degree or not. Given the dramatic expansion of higher education in the past three decades, that distinction has become much less relevant. The other real divisions are between north and south and between those who attended private school and those who did not. Unless you are a politician, the communities further north than Oxford in the west and York in the east appear to be of little interest or importance. One of my friends, when I asked him about his new neighbors, said, *sotto voce*, "They're perfectly all right — but they *are* from Birmingham, you know." And I often have the impression that my friends living in London and the southwest think of Wales and Scotland — which are even further afield — as quaint, rather unusual countries that have little in common with life as

Highly Skilled Migrant

it is lived in England. (The Glaswegian accent in particular is considered a linguistic abomination.)

Many private schools in England, some of which are still confusingly called "public," remain the training grounds for proper pronunciation, even if the days of clipped and snooty "received pronunciation" are now behind us. The era of the hallowed grammar school — the stepping-stone for so many successful academics and politicians — is also well behind us, replaced by a mixture of "comprehensives" and local "academies." Even with the recent increase in fees at British universities, they remain a bargain compared to the cost of a private college education in the United States, and it is therefore little wonder that parents (and grandparents) pay as much as £35,000 a year to send children to private schools. This is their most precious investment, and it is one that is usually social as well as educational. Although only seven percent of English children attend private schools, they eventually make up a disproportionate cohort of undergraduates at the premier universities — and within the upper echelons of the cabinet, the diplomatic service, and Whitehall. Bath alone is home to five independent schools (King Edward's, Monkton Combe, Kingswood, Prior Park, and the Royal High School), and one of the two premier Catholic "colleges," Downside, is only twenty-five minutes away. Marlborough, Eton, Winchester, and Sherborn are within easy striking distance, and it is still the practice for some families to send their children away at the age of seven. One of my female friends once told me that she was perfectly happy as an English wife because she knew exactly where she stood in her husband's affections: in roughly third or fourth place, behind his schoolmates, his nanny, and his horse and dogs.

There is also a strong bond among those who have served in the British armed forces, and what I have found surprising is how fully those who are currently serving in the military are woven into the social lives of civilians. Uniformed soldiers and naval officers are often included in private events, and the annual Thanksgiving dinner hosted by the American Society in London is in fact a tribute to the armed forces of both countries. Whereas military men, women, and their families are usually located (even isolated) in communities of their own in America, this is largely not the case here. The Military and Naval Club (the much-loved "In and Out") and the Army and Navy Club are located across from each other in St. James's Square in London, and both include large numbers of civilians among their members. Military service is respected in Britain to a degree that must seem peculiar to many within American society, and there is still more than a hint of romance attached to the military here, especially to those equestrian regiments — the Royal Horse Guards or the Household Cavalry, for instance — that have seen centuries of service to the nation.

A career in the military, especially as an officer, is one secure path to upward social mobility, but the campaign for and against remaining in the European Union in 2016 revealed the extent to which Britain remains a bifurcated and class-conscious nation. Those with university degrees were firmly in the "Remain" camp (70 percent) whereas 62 percent of those who had only earned basic qualifications in school were committed to "Leave." There was a wide divide between those in the city (Remain) and those in the country (Leave), and an equally wide gap between those in the highest social classes and those in the lowest. In many ways the decision to leave the EU was a protest vote: a protest against indifferent politicians in Westminster, European regulation, unbridled immigration, and the ever-widening chasm between the haves and the have-nots. I've been reminded during my time here of those lines from Benjamin Disraeli's *Sybil*, which we read as freshmen at Williams: Britain, he wrote, was essentially "two nations … between whom there is no intercourse and no sympathy; who are as ignorant of each other's habits, thoughts, and feelings, as if they were dwellers in different zones." The current state of affairs is clearly not this bleak, but the new government formed in 2016 has inherited serious problems that must be addressed.

Because of these changes within society during the past several decades, those features of British life that have remained fairly constant have provided me, at least, with a sense of amusement as well as continuity. Acting remains one of this country's strongest traditions, and Bath boasts a Theatre Royal that showcases many plays before they make their official debut in the West End. My tailor in Marylebone is Scandinavian, which makes him more English than the English when it comes to menswear, which suits me just fine. Sunday roast lunch (12:45 until 4) was first a rite of passage for me and now a source of real pleasure — although I still have not mastered the art of smashing my food against the wrong side of my fork. Drinks parties, garden parties, book launch parties, dinner parties with live musical entertainment, significant birthdays and anniversaries: these are all warm and engaging occasions, and Bathonians, at least, make the most of them. Having a large circle of friends, moreover, has turned out to be one of the nicest surprises "little England" has afforded me so far. I relish their dry sense of humor, the resignation to recent or impending disaster, and even their habit of deflating rather than praising their friends when good tidings — a knighthood, for instance — comes someone's way. This same spirit of bantering carries over into the workplace as well, and although my colleagues' approach to goals and deadlines may appear to be more casual than I was used to in the United States, those deadlines and goals are always well met. As an American, moreover, I seem to have been granted a "pass" of some kind. Because I cannot be precisely placed on the social scale based on my accent or manners, I must therefore be taken for what I am — although having attended Oxford certainly helps.

The cultural amenities in Britain remain remarkable for a nation of this size, moreover, and what I have found most satisfying is the seriousness with which writers and artists are treated here. It is true that this country has become something of a celebrity culture peopled by footballers, rock stars, and television personalities, but the amount of coverage devoted to literature and the arts remains unusually high. Bath nourishes two independent bookstores, both of which host numerous readings, and this activity is compounded not only in London but in cities throughout the country. Book and music festivals are almost too numerous to count let alone to attend, and the highlights of some of them — the summer Proms in London or the annual Hay Literary Festival not far from Bath, for example — are given extended coverage on both radio and television. I cannot imagine an American television network even mentioning the winners of various literary awards unless it is that elusive Nobel prize, whereas the BBC provides live coverage of the announcement of both the Costa and Man Booker prize winners each year.

The New Yorker used to run a small notice at the bottom of the page entitled "There Will Always Be An England." Most of the newspaper reports reproduced there focused on English men and women giving artificial respiration to injured hedgehogs. I trust that there *will* always be an England, one in which half of the women are (or were) named Liz, Sarah, Emma, or Sue, and in which the men are (or were) given names that you will rarely come across in the United States: Simon, Rupert, Robin, Nigel, Adrian, Julian, Anthony, Ian, Colin, Miles, Giles, Florian, Finbar, Gareth, Noel, Maximilian, Peregrine, and Valerian (okay, the last two are dukes, but still . . .).

CHAPTER ELEVEN

Good Taste Costs No More

My parents did not have a very well-stocked library. My father had some books devoted to business matters, my mother a collection of "condensed" books from the Reader's Digest. There were a few titles that looked intriguing (*Atlas Shrugged*, for instance), but nothing that I can remember taking with me up to my bedroom to read. When my mother purchased a copy of James Michener's *Hawaii*, I was the second to make my way through it, proudly telling my parents and brother, as they watched a program on television in the evening, that it took me twenty-four hours to read it. "That's too long a period to spend reading," my father said, barely looking up from the television set. Well of course it was — but I had been reading it for almost two weeks, I hastened to say.

One title on those shelves in the living room did pique my interest, however, and although I never took it down to read it, I keenly remember its title and the lesson it intended to impart: *Good Taste Costs No More*. I took that admonition as something of a challenge, thinking about how my parents' house was furnished, trying to make intelligent distinctions between one item of clothing and another in the department store in which I worked on Monday evening and on Saturday each week. It seemed to make sense to me: if two or three objects cost the same amount of money, surely one could choose which one was the more attractive or of better quality.

My parents did have reasonably good taste, after all, even though it was certainly of the Midwestern, mid-century variety. They had no family heirlooms to speak of. When I was a student at Oxford, they stayed in a nearby hostelry called The Old Parsonage, where my father attempted — much to my embarrassment — to purchase an antique umbrella stand that he fancied. The owner rightly refused to part with it, but the next time I visited Cedar Rapids I noticed that quite a similar object now stood in their hallway. When I asked my father about it, he proudly told me that the store carpenter had made it for him and that "it was better than the one in Oxford." "How so?" I asked. "Because it's new," he replied.

I think that my parents purchased the prints in the living room — rather nice, hand-colored views of coastal scenes in Britain — from the department store as well, although they also bought at least one oil by a local painter, whose name I have forgotten even though it was always mentioned in reverential tones. (They spoke in hushed voices about Baker furniture as well.) The outside of their house was more impressive than the interior, including a wide veranda on the front, a long driveway that led to a *porte-cochère* off the back of the building, and a turn-around that led to a two-story garage, styled in the same red brick and boasting a chauffeur's apartment on the second floor. Richard Gere decided to live in the house, located on Grande Avenue, when he was filming *Miles from Home* in Cedar Rapids in the late 1980s. It was not a grande house, but it had decent bones and was nicely situated on a small hill. There were bats in the attic and a but-

2330 GRANDE AVENUE S. E.

ler's buzzer beneath the dining-room table, which my brother and I pressed so often that my harried mother finally had it removed.

Although I was not, like Charles Ryskamp, subscribing to auction catalogues from Sotheby Parke-Benet when I was a teenager, I did grasp the fact that I had an interest in the environment in which I lived. Four years in college were largely a holding period, but in my second year at Oxford I was able to rent the top floor of a Stuart manor house just outside the city, not far from Bladen and Woodstock. My wife Barbara and I originally leased it with another American couple, but that relationship soured, our friends departed, and I was in the difficult position of not having enough money to pay the entire rent. "No matter," the kind owner of the estate told me; "you are a gentleman, so just continue to give me what you're already paying." That was a close call — and a rather surprising compliment to a young American at the time — for I would have dreaded leaving that magical setting before the end of my second year. I can still spot the house, Yarnton Manor, from the train line that runs between Oxford and Banbury, and my memory of my time there blends in nicely with images of all of those libraries and donnish rooms that I frequented as part of my time at the university. And when Charles Ryskamp made it possible to live on Grace Lambert's estate on the outskirts of Princeton two years later, I felt that lightning had struck twice, and I therefore tried to take advantage of it, realizing that the interiors of her house might well have been described in the pages of *The Spoils of Poynton*.

    I've already written about my interest in old-master prints and in the slow process, when I lived in Chicago, of training my eye so that engravings by Hogarth might give way to good impressions of etchings by Piranesi. That's part of the enterprise of refining one's taste — and once that has begun, it's rarely possible for better taste to cost no more, as I quickly discovered. Chicago offered another source of visual and tactile refinement, located in that behemoth of a building known as the Merchandise Mart, the largest building in America (I was told) before the construction of the Pentagon. My father had taken us to the Mart when we were young, and he very kindly helped me purchase a leather sofa there when I was first setting up an apartment with Barbara in Chicago. I wanted a Chesterfield, of course, with all of its studs and padding, but I had to settle for something more modern and less grand, eventually scratched to death by two children and three golden retrievers.

    I really owed my long-term relationship with the Merchandise Mart to Bob and Gloria Turner, however, the owners of a chic shop in Old Town that specialized in furniture and lighting. Bob and Gloria are both Midwesterners, they have very good taste, and Bob included his services as an interior designer with the cost of his furniture. That made good sense to me and to my second wife, Diana, given our resources, and we happily showed Bob the apartment in the sky — like a Mies van der Rohe but not quite a Mies van der Rohe — that was in need of his advice and encouragement. We agreed on the furniture and layout, he smiled upon the antiques and prints that I had collected (he said of the eight engravings of *The Rake's Progress*, "they make a statement"), and he gave me *carte blanche* at the Merchandise Mart. He also encouraged me not to take all of his strictures as holy doctrine. He had discovered that one of his clients had traced chalk lines around each of the objects he had set out on tables in her rooms so that they would always be in the right place.

But when I finally asked Bob and Gloria over for dinner and a chance to see the final result, I could sense more than a little coolness in the air. I thought that I had followed his advice in principle as carefully as I could, but when I dropped by his shop a few days later to see what the matter was, he simply said, "You didn't leave the walls white." No, I didn't! I worked for over a month with the son of my secretary in the dean's office at Northwestern, a master paint mixer, to create what we finally called "the perfect taupe." And we were ahead of the curve at the time, for taupe is out of fashion as often as it is in. I thought that taupe gave the crisp, modern space — dark floors, hard edges, wrap-around windows running from floor to ceiling — more definition and just a modicum of warmth. But somehow I had violated an unspoken modernist pact, and I had precious little time (or interest) in painting the entire apartment white again.

I did have an interest, however, in making the Merchandise Mart my second home. During a sabbatical year, partly to punctuate the long days spent working on what would become *The Elements of Life*, I often (okay, very often) drove my car down to the Mart and explored the extraordinary assemblage of antiques, fabric, furniture, lighting, and rug boutiques. The doormen knew to let me in, and I went there so often that everyone, I think, simply took me to be a new interior decorator. I was offered swatches and paint wheels and invitations to drinks parties, all of which I happily accepted. And outside the Mart, on the side away from the river, a fairly large neighborhood of antiques shops and art galleries had suddenly mushroomed into place, and I carefully made my way through this exotic bazaar as well. And it was in one of those venues that I eventually made one of the two major purchases in my career as a collector.

Leslie Hindman Auctioneers had opened its doors shortly before I stumbled upon it, and I therefore found myself looking at a collection of objects that must have been part of its second or third sale. That was a good state of affairs because the furniture and rugs were really quite fine and not all of the savvy dealers and collectors had made their way there yet. I was pleasantly struck by many things during my first visit — and later on as well, when I successfully bid on a Regency chair of Cuban mahogany and two lovely Persian rugs — but what caught my fancy during that first preview was a simple portrait of a woman in full profile. It had a tacky frame on it, but the canvas was in good condition and the sitter's lacework and face were beautifully painted. It reminded me a bit of those many self-portraits by Angelica Kauffman, and when I opened the catalogue and found the right number, sure enough, the portrait was attributed to Kauffman and bore a surprisingly low estimate, even though it was a very high number for me.

The auction would not take place for several days, and so I twice made my way to the Ryerson Library at the Art Institute, consulted the rather spotty scholarship devoted to Kauffman, and worked through all of the auction sales that contained examples of her work. There wasn't much information available, but after talking with the staff at Leslie Hindman and educating my eye as best I could, I thought that the following facts could be established. The painting was attributed to Kauffman but it was not signed. If it were indeed a genuine work of her hand, then it was the only portrait in full profile that she ever painted (not a good sign). The label indicated that the sitter was "Sarah Harrod," but that surname looked like wishful thinking and I was able to establish that she was in fact Sarah Harrop, the leading soprano on the London stage at the end of the eighteenth century. She married John Bates, an impresario, and had been painted by Kauffman in a formal, iconographical format in a picture that had disappeared from scholarly view. Only an engraving of that painting remained, and I discovered that one of those prints had sold at Colnaghi in London for more than the low estimate on my painting in Chicago. (That was a good sign.)

Kauffman had kept sitters' books, especially during her years in Rome, but I couldn't, at the time, determine whether they had been published anywhere. The painting had come to the auction house from the estate of the late Mrs. McCormick, the widow of the legendary Colonel McCormick, the owner of the *Chicago Tribune* and an heir to the

Good Taste Costs No More

fortune generated by McCormick's reaper. The painting had been purchased for her by a nephew at Sotheby's in London in the late 1960s and had, like a Goya also hanging in her living room overlooking Lake Michigan, had its background painted over (in green) so that the works of art blended in with her color scheme. The Kauffman had been successfully cleaned; the Goya, on the other hand, had been ruined.

That's what I knew. If I bid on her, I was taking a risk, but the painting was a very good one and I decided to trust my eye, placing a bid at the lower estimate and deciding not to attend the auction. I felt almost physically ill after doing this, for I had bid every cent that I had in the bank, the proceeds of the sale of a weekend house that I had shared with my former wife and another couple. I waited with discomfort until the results of the auction were known: the painting, I discovered, had sold at the low estimate — and I had been the only bidder. A few days later I felt even more uncomfortable and decided to put the painting in the back of my station wagon and run it down to the Art Institute, where I had arranged for Rick Brettell to see it. The Art Institute's curator of paintings came to our meeting armed with an ultraviolet lamp, examined every inch of the canvas closely, pronounced the painting to be a good one (although he couldn't verify the attribution), and recommended that I put a decent frame on it. Which I did, at some cost.

Later, when I moved to Boston, I asked my friend Wendy Roworth to take a look at it over lunch one day. As one of the world's experts on Kauffman, she had been dubious about the attribution because of the full-profile pose, but once she saw the painting in the flesh she quickly smiled and said that yes, it was the real thing. Angela Rosenthal at Dartmouth liked what she saw as well, and gave me the name of the country house in Ireland where the other painting of Sarah Harrop was hanging. Later, both an expert at Christie's and Robert Holden, a private dealer, travelled to Bath to look at it, and both thought that it was "right." But the most difficult test of all remained, and thus three years ago I wrapped the painting up and took it on the train to London, where it was to be examined by the rather terrifying scholar preparing Kauffman's *catalogue raisonné*, Bettina Baumgärtel. I dropped the picture off in a friend's office, was formally introduced to Dr. Baumgärtel and her two assistants (a conservator and a photographer), and was told to go away until the late afternoon. This didn't look good. But when I retrieved the painting later that day — another day of discomfort produced by this Georgian beauty — I was told by someone in the office that it looked promising and that the picture had been photographed. A day later I received an email with the good news: despite the unusual pose, Bettina Baumgärtel had smiled upon my youthful purchase. So it was now official: after many peregrinations on my part, and after meticulous examination by four experts, the portrait I had fallen in love with (and sacrificed a good deal to retain) was a legitimate Angelica Kauffman, and the only one of its kind.

Good Taste Costs No More

Kauffman died in Rome, the recipient of a rather extravagant funeral service and procession in the Eternal City, and it was in Rome that I discovered the other major object that I decided I had to have. I think that I had first seen one in the pages of *Architectural Digest*, probably in the section in the front of the magazine devoted to interesting shops in what (at the time) might have been presented as rather exotic locations to an American audience. It was a dining-room table made up of a sheet of glass balanced on top of two marble struts. The one I saw in the magazine featured a black steel rod that linked the two struts together, just under the canopy of the heavy glass. Perfect, I thought. I was heading to Rome, my friend and colleague Leonard Barkan was living there that year, certainly he could help me find such a simple and beautiful object. So I was in touch with Leonard, he asked around, and he was told that we should take a stroll down the Via Coronari once I arrived. When we did, we soon discovered a shop entirely devoted to such tables in various sizes and in various grades and colors of marble, most of them sporting rather hefty price tags. I immediately saw what I wanted: the simplest one of all, just glass, the black steel rod, and two carved Travertine struts that dated from the eighteenth century. Although it was expensive, it was the cheapest table in the shop, and after speaking to the elderly woman who ran the business, Leonard told me that we should take our leave and reconnoiter.

The problem, he explained, was that she didn't want to sell her table to an American. And, he added, "when I told her, in my best Italian, that we were both professors of English in Chicago, she gave me a scowl that had 'Mafia' written all over it." But, Leonard went on, "let me come back again and see if someone else also looks after the shop. Maybe we'll find someone who doesn't think we're in the *Cosa Nostra*." And that's how it played out. Leonard visited the shop when the woman's son was there, they hit it off, the table was available to be shipped to Chicago — but there would be no discount in price. I gritted my teeth and agreed to the sum, asked Leonard to measure the size of the glass so that I wouldn't have to ship it to America, and arranged to have the money transferred from our account to his. And then, because the tourist business was so slow that winter, Alitalia decided to remove seats from some of its planes and make its money by taking on more cargo.

A week later the Travertine struts were waiting for me in the customs office near O'Hare airport. The official there was not very obliging, however. He was a rough-and-tumble Chicagoan of the old school, and he took the bill of lading for the shipment and asked me to read it to him. I did: it simply said "2 Travertine blocks" in Italian. "How do I know these are antique?" he asked. "It doesn't say that they are antique." Well, I replied, if you look at the name of the shipper, you will see that it was an antiques shop. That still didn't do much good, so I put it to him this way: "Why would I pay to ship two pieces of marble thousands of miles if they weren't very old and very special? It would have been much cheaper to go to the suburbs and have them made brand new, wouldn't it?" He thought for a moment and then agreed, warning me to get the right kind of documentation next time. A week or two later the glass had been made to order, the struts and glass were delivered to our door, and I was ready to put the table on view and seat Leonard at it when he returned home from the Campo dei Fiori.

That table has served many purposes and has been put to good use in many dining rooms and studies during the past thirty years. It was shown to best advantage, however, when I had the local movers in Bath transport it once again, this time to the top of Lansdown Hill. I made the move from Boston to England at the beginning of 2010, and for the first two years I rented quite a nice flat not too far from Pulteney Bridge, which had been designed by Robert Adam. The address was actually grander than the building itself: Connaught Mansions had served over the past two centuries as a long row of terrace houses, then as a hotel, then as offices for the Royal Navy during the Second World War, and then as the local council's office for drivers' licenses and drivers' tests. Some of the new friends who visited me there still had unpleasant memories of having to show up at the building to take their first road tests. In order to reach me, you had to climb two flights of stairs and then walk through six fire doors until, a block later, you knocked on my door. The flat was nicely located and had just enough room to accommodate me, but I was not allowed to

Good Taste Costs No More

paint the walls — to "decorate" them, as the English confusingly say — and I felt more than a little constricted as I began to make a home for myself back in the mother country.

Like so many other things in my new life in England, the ascent to Lansdown Crescent began in the men's locker room at the Bath Spa Hotel. The first person I met there was Michael Whitcroft, who, upon hearing that I was an eighteenth-century scholar, directed my attention to the flat that he and his wife Sandie had inherited from her mother. It had too few bedrooms for them, he said, and it wouldn't be long before they would move down Lansdown Hill to the handsome house they had recently purchased, not far from where I was leasing my first apartment. Michael thought that I should rent it from them when they moved. What they had not reckoned on, however, was the glacial pace at which the local planning authority approves any changes to historically significant buildings — and Bath is nothing but historically significant buildings, including the flat from which they were attempting to depart.

Anyone who visits Bath soon succumbs to the Georgian splendor of these buildings, each one of them erected in the neoclassical style and clad in the honey-colored stone for which the area is famous. If you had a bird's-eye view as well as some sturdy walking shoes, you would immediately sense the elegant geometry with which John Wood (father and son) laid out the city almost 300 years ago: long boulevards (Great Pulteney Street, where I first lived), ample parks (Henrietta Gardens), formal squares (Queen's), dramatic circles (the King's Circus), long winding thoroughfares (the Paragon), and the distinctive crescents that mark each level of the city's many hills (Royal, Cavendish, Norfolk, Camden, Lansdown). It was to this last crescent, the highest of them all, that I was eventually headed.

By contemplating such a move, I was following in the footsteps of William Beckford, but Beckford had traveled far — and famously lived elsewhere — before he finally, and permanently, landed on Lansdown. He was the son of the richest man in England, a London merchant who traded in slaves and other "commodities" in the West Indies in the middle of the eighteenth century. Beckford had every advantage the Augustan age in England could afford a prodigious *arriviste*: private tutors (Mozart gave him music lessons), the obligatory Grand Tour, a torrid affair with another young man (which eventually prevented him from snagging a peerage), a wife who remained loyal to her complicated and often cantankerous husband, and ample funds to collect whatever his heart desired — and his heart desired the best of just about everything.

In the literary world, Beckford is best known for his short novel entitled *Vathek*, a pan-sexual Gothic romance that was translated from the French and edited for a modern audience by one of my tutors at Oxford, Roger Lonsdale. I had therefore read Beckford — and learned about his creation of the extravagant Fonthill Abbey — at a fairly young age, but it is as a collector that Beckford has remained best known, both when he filled Fonthill with the fruits of his many trips to the Continent and then, facing tougher financial circumstances, "sold up" and moved the remnants of his collection to Lansdown: paintings, statues, prints and drawings, coins and medals, all of those objects which we place under the sign of *virtù*.

Good Taste Costs No More

In 1824 Beckford purchased No. 20 on the crescent, the last townhouse on the western side, as well as No. 1 Lansdown Place West, the first townhouse across a small mews entrance. He linked the two houses by building a bridge between them at the second-floor level and eventually made that space into a library. The elevation at No. 20 didn't mesh very well with No. 1, however, and Beckford decided to sell Lansdown West, bricking up the west end of the bridge — and then, several years later, purchasing No. 19 on the other side and creating his famous Grecian library on the ground floor there.

The Grecian library is perhaps better known than the bridge, largely because the diarist James Lees-Milne worked and wrote there for many years, but the flat my friends inherited includes the *pièce de résistance* of the entire confabulation: Beckford's picture gallery, which measured 43 by 28 feet, with an elaborate 16-foot ceiling and important paintings by Raphael, Bellini, Velázquez, and other old masters hanging on its walls (many of them now hang on the walls of the National Gallery in London). Beckford is said to have referred to it as "The Duchess of Hamilton's State Apartment," ostensibly in honor of his daughter but essentially (and characteristically) in honor of himself.

At the beginning of the 1980s, the townhouse was converted into five flats on five floors and the picture gallery was cut down (quite effectively so) in order to create a second bedroom and a second bath, but the reception room itself still measures 31 by 28 feet and is among the largest private rooms in Bath. When friends entered it for the first time, I almost always experienced a second or two of stunned silence, occasionally followed by an expletive: "Bloody hell" from the English, "Holy shit" from the Americans. Even my jaded twenty-three-year-old son simply nodded his head as he pronounced his verdict: "Cool, Dad."

So, weighing in at almost 900 square feet, the gallery remained quite an imposing space, and my challenge was therefore two-fold: how to live up to William Beckford, the greatest aesthete of his age, while also making the room warm and inviting. How, in other words, to blend the elegant with the comfortable — and on a strict budget, no less. My first solution was to paint over the cream-colored walls and pull the room together, adding warmth along with a strong neutral background for the Georgian furniture and my collection of Piranesis. I chose a rich yellow with the confusing name of "Light Buff" (you can only imagine what "Dark Buff" is like), a color that looks almost like apricot early in the morning and then turns almost gold as day slowly shades into evening.

 My second gambit was to break up the vast space by fashioning three distinct areas: a small sitting space as you enter, my dining-room table of glass and Roman Travertine in the bay overlooking the street, and a large sitting area in front of the fireplace (not Beckford's mantle piece, by the way, but perfectly acceptable). The center was punctuated by a round table of English yew that I have carted from one house and apartment to another for more than two decades. And then the small, playful surprises: two articulated lay figures seated on the three-bay bookcase; the Portuguese processional figure, draped in eighteenth-century silk by a local doll-maker; and the pristine miniature "Bath chair" whose wavy glass and upholstery date it to the late nineteenth century — and purchased, I should add,

Good Taste Costs No More

at the Saturday-morning flea market in Bath that also yielded the 13-foot Hamadan rug on the floor of the bridge.

My third decision was simply one of aesthetic restraint as I resisted my initial inclination to hang as many of the Piranesis as possible in place of Beckford's Raphaels and Bellinis. The introduction of the rich yellow coloring not only served as a foil to the intricate swags and cartouches of the cornice-work, but it also managed to give the entire room a sense of being furnished already. Instead of double-hanging (or even triple-hanging) the prints on the walls, I therefore mounted only ten of them, strategically spaced around the room: two of the great, dark etchings from the famous series of imaginary prisons, a rare *grottescho*, the artist's only architectural plan (never built, alas), Roman views and scenes of Tivoli, and two early etchings from Piranesi's first book, devoted to architecture and perspective.

This exercise in self-restraint continued into the bedroom, which led onto the bridge. These walls were also painted in Light Buff, two more large etchings by Piranesi graced the space above my bed, and the portrait of Sarah Harrop looked down upon me as I slept. Two indented bookcases, supplied with glass shelving, posed a potentially nasty problem, for the cases were too shallow to hold any actual books and I try to keep my collection of "smalls" grouped together on wooden surfaces. But a little tinkering with the shelves provided me with space — for the first time in a long time — to display my CDs in alphabetical order as well as a number of my smaller prints, including an etching by Kauffman taken from a painting by Guercino.

And then there was the famous bridge, a Grade-I listed space in its own right although some of its history remains somewhat murky. Our current thinking is that the oak-and-walnut bookcases on the back wall of the bridge were imported from Fonthill Abbey after Beckford sold it. They mesh very nicely with the frames of the two doors and with the three windows on the front side, which look down upon the street and the pasture beyond it. The huge mirror at the end of the bridge was a bit daunting, so I placed my desk in front of it, fortified the table with a small collection of marble obelisks, and hung my Scottish landscape painting by Frances Stoddart above it. The combination of objects provided a focal point for the eye, and given the fact that the *enfilade* stretching from the fireplace to the end of the bridge is seventy feet long, a focal point was very much needed.

Flexing my sense of self-control had led to several problems, however. Although my previous flat was significantly smaller than this one in the sheer number of square feet, it actually offered more hanging space on its walls. Where, precisely, were all of the rest of my prints going to find an appropriate home? Some migrated to my office at the museum; some had to be placed in the large drawers on the bridge

Good Taste Costs No More

that housed Beckford's collection of coins and medals; and some, I'm afraid, turned the back bathroom into a miniature gallery with nine Piranesis on the walls, my best Persian runner on the floor, and a Hieronymus Cock hung over the door. The hallway accommodated a few more prints and the kitchen served a similar purpose. I painted the back bedroom a rich terracotta in order to complement another small trove of Piranesis and — more importantly — my collection of title-pages to Sir William Hamilton's four-volume publication of his

Greek and Etruscan vases. All of the rooms on the back of the flat — bathroom, kitchen, and the spare bedroom — looked down on a large and beautifully maintained garden, at the end of which Beckford created the trail that led up to his tower at the top of Lansdown Hill. The trail has all but disappeared, the tower has been successfully restored at great expense, and Beckford's huge granite funeral casket remains in place in the cemetery adjoining the tower. Beckford's devoted followers, who remain legion, make their pilgrimage to the tower and to the crescent throughout the year. Rarely a day went by when I didn't discover someone standing in front of the bridge and taking a photograph. And in the spring and summer, the ewes and their lovely lambs in the pasture attracted an additional stream of hardy sightseers.

Would Beckford have approved of what I had done to his legendary spaces? I highly doubt it. Moderation and aesthetic restraint had little place in his world. The five large windows in his picture gallery and the three on the bridge were all hung with red velvet curtains during his lifetime. Bookcases encircled the gallery at waist height and I imagine that the walls were heavily papered if not heavily flocked. The collector who looked down his nose at the items on sale in the auction devoted to Horace Walpole's acquisitions at Strawberry Hill — but who nevertheless purchased quite a few of them, bidding against his son-in-law, the Duke of Hamilton — would surely not have condescended to approve of anything that I've collected over the years. But all of the pictures and prints and most of the furniture that I placed there were created during Beckford's lifetime, and that much (at least) we had in common. But whereas Beckford was notoriously reclusive in the final decades of his life, I cherished the opportunity to put these rooms to good use by entertaining my friends on a regular basis. The picture gallery, in particular, had "party" written all over it: drinks party, dinner party, book launch party, even a private recital such as Yehudi Menuhin was supposed to have given in the room a few decades earlier.

While I lived there, I spent some time thinking about the opportunity I was enjoying of inserting my life into the spaces formerly occupied by my illustrious predecessor. There was supposed to be a ghost, but if it exists, I never met it. I made a point of re-reading my books on neoclassicism, of which Beckford was a late exemplar, and I was struck by Mario Praz's remark, almost a contemptuous aside, made seventy-five years ago: "Neoclassicism is a phenomenon which I would rather feel intuitively than judge; most people hasten to judge it without waiting to know whether they can feel it." Given the history of those rooms, the setting, the dimensions, the views, I had no trouble hosting those intuitive feelings. I judged the phenomenon of neoclassical decoration to fit quite comfortably into my own trajectory from middle-class Midwestern interiors to an early seventeenth-century manor house, from a gardener's cottage in Princeton to a modern glass box high above Chicago's Lincoln Park, from an apartment on Boston's Beacon Hill to a proper house on Boston's South Shore — and thence to the environs of Bath and eventually to Lansdown Crescent. The eccentric aesthete Stephen Tennant once wrote that "the exact limitations of one's taste should be an intense pleasure." I continue to enjoy the playful enigma of that statement. One's taste can change, of course, and those limitations can expand, but I continue to relish Tennant's focus on the pleasure to be found just on the periphery of one's comfort zone.

I have written about my time on Lansdown in the past tense, for two years after I had made that pilgrimage (and had substantially re-decorated the flat) my friends decided to place it on the market. I wasn't entirely surprised; it was a risk I had been willing to take, although I wish I could have stayed there a few years longer. I quickly moved down to a maisonette near the Royal Crescent (a much more central location) and then, a year later, down into the city proper once again, to a garden flat (with a garden), situated across a small park from where Jane Austen and Thomas de Quincey used to live — although not together, of course. That side of the park had been destroyed by Hitler's *Luftwaffe* during three retaliatory strikes he ordered after the Allied forces had bombed Heidelberg. But my row of terrace houses is still standing, and Sarah Harrop and company have a very nice home there indeed.

I've now lived on my own for almost eight years after living with

Richard Wendorf

Barbara, then Diana, and then Elizabeth over four entire decades. This transition continues to feel surprisingly comfortable rather than odd or even strange. Part of that sense of comfort derives from knowing, at this point in my life, what my basic requirements are, how all of those books and prints should be organized, and the extent to which those various collections have become very much a part of that life. In making my transition to England, I've moved four times in less than six years, a practice that I don't recommend to anyone. But making such domestic peregrinations has given me immense pleasure as well as the usual headaches and precarious bank accounts — not least because I enjoy the process of thinking about how various pieces of furniture or art are going to work best in their next home. The objects remain roughly the same. I try not to purchase new pieces simply to suit a new space, although this is sometimes necessary. I believe in buying objects that are "right" on their own terms, no matter where they may be placed. And thus much of the pleasure lies in determining how those new juxtapositions will work.

My spouses and partners have been, for the most part, willing to put up with such shifting about — and they have supported me (in spirit, and sometimes in cash) as I've contemplated purchases large and small. Barbara and I started out from scratch and ended up with some lovely pieces of furniture and some handsome prints. Diana's mother had a remarkable eye, and I think that I learned as much from studying the design of her home in Tucson as from dining at Grace Lambert's house in Princeton. Diana has become a collector herself and was not appalled when I set my heart first on a Georgian painting and then on that glass-and-Travertine table. As a paper conservator, Elizabeth took as much interest in my print collection as I did — although always from a different and enlightening angle. Liz Wildi worked with me on the design of the garden that graces the back of my rather unusual garden flat — and planted it entirely in green and white. These partners have become collaborators and co-conspirators, and yet I remain the one who continually sets the wheels in motion.

At some point I shall have to stop moving, but I doubt that I shall ever entirely lose interest in creating interiors that my friends will

Good Taste Costs No More

consider to be sufficiently "smart" and comfortable at the same time. And I have discovered an alternative to this constant to-ing and fro-ing, one that allows for almost infinite creativity and pleasure, so allow me to digress for a moment to set the scene. Although I worked reasonably hard at both Oxford and Princeton, I often found that I needed a palliative to the routine of graduate studies, something that would provide a maximum amount of entertainment with a minimum amount of effort. Yes, there was tennis and squash and even cricket at Oxford, but there was also the relatively unexplored world of English detective fiction. As a child I had read the Hardy Boys, and later on I discovered the pleasures of Sherlock Holmes, but the fiction of Michael Innes, Edmund Crispin, Dorothy Sayers, Margery Allingham, Ruth Rendell, Colin Dexter — and many others — was a marvelous surprise. I naturally toyed with the idea of writing something myself. I decided to center it on a case of old-fashioned identity theft among Americans studying at Oxford, and I came up with a title, *The Subtle Thief*, based on a line in one of Milton's sonnets: "Time, the subtle thief of youth." But I had no cast of characters, nor a serious plot, nor a sense of how I should write the work, in the first person or in the third. Time quickly slipped by for me as well, and although I took up the novels of Rex Stout and Amanda Cross and Ross Macdonald when I lived in Princeton, I was no wiser about what to do with my still inchoate thoughts.

Then, nine years ago, I was coaxed into a spinning class at my fitness center near Boston and then into a charity "ride" — which is a euphemism for a marathon — from Quincy down to Provincetown on the far tip of Cape Cod. I had six months of training and then a two-day, 150-mile cycling trek ahead of me, and because cycling is such a solitary sport, I had a good deal of time to think about a number of issues in my life, including the way in which successful detective fiction seems to work. At the heart of many of the most successful series, I realized, was the give and take between two central characters: think of Holmes and Watson, Nero Wolfe and Archie Goodwin, or Nick and Nora Charles, enshrined in all of those "Thin Man" films of the 1930s and 1940s. How could I capitalize on that dynamic and bring it up to date at the same time? That was the challenge I set myself as I trained on the lonely back roads of Scituate, Cohasset, and Hull.

The answer (or at least one answer), it dawned on me, was to make the two protagonists romantic partners who continually sparred with one another, a bit like the old Tracy and Hepburn coupling and uncoupling, and yet much more sexually explicit — and set within the art world of New York City. Nick would become Nicky Higginson, a Boston Brahmin novelist happily living in bohemian exile in Manhattan; her partner — in what might be an intriguingly open relationship — would be the art historian and connoisseur Desmond Fairbrother. Nicky would tell the tale; Desi would solve the mystery; together they would enjoy — and expose — the privileges and pretensions of the glittering world of collectors, curators, writers, galleristas, and interior designers, packaged (for the most part) in the Hamptons and the Upper East Side.

Once I had my template and had experimented with writing from a liberated woman's perspective, the novels seemed to write themselves. First *The Subtle Thief*, of course, which is a tale of unmasking; and then *The Man Who Looked Too Closely*, which hinges on forgery in the art world. I have called them "entertainments" in a light-handed gesture, but they actually bend the contours of traditional detective fiction in two important ways: first, by beginning as comedies of manners that only become genuine mysteries halfway through the narrative; and second, by leaving the reader at the end of the novel — and even Nicky and Desi, for that matter — uncertain of whether a murder actually took place. I have also written half of a third entertainment, *The Upside-Down House*, in which Desi is accused of murder following a sexual escapade in the Hamptons, and Nicky and her friends must therefore undertake the task of detection themselves. Upside-down indeed.

But the house in this third fiction is upside-down as well, a beach house that must be inverted in order to provide views over the Southampton dunes to the ocean beyond — and the creation of appropriate buildings and interiors is crucial to the atmospheric effects I have tried to produce in this entire series of books. Desi inherits a con-

Good Taste Costs No More

verted carriage house in which he entertains the great and the not-so-good. Nicky enjoys a studio apartment a few blocks away as well as an old sea captain's clapboard house in Sag Harbor. The conception and construction of the upside-down house provide the visual and narrative background for the third entertainment and enable me, as the actual designer, to create a home in which I shall never live. These, I have found, are some of the pleasures of writing this kind of fiction: not just experiments with voice and dialogue or the adjustments of character, but the opportunity as well to imagine new spaces and the new collections that will be placed there. Writing these entertainments has allowed me to stretch the boundaries of my own taste, to do it for free, and perhaps even to profit from it when these works finally take published form, either in print or in the brave new world of electronic media. In this sense, at least, good taste can cost no more.

CHAPTER TWELVE

Sitting for One's Picture

Part of the brief for a library or museum director is to give talks about one's institution and the books and works of art housed within it, particularly objects that have recently entered the collection. I've always enjoyed this form of presentation, which began with talks for the Visiting Committee at Harvard and then for an enthusiastic group of supporters each year at the Boston Athenæum. But I've also grown to relish a somewhat different challenge during the past few years in England. Each spring the Royal Society of Portrait Painters holds its annual exhibition at the Mall Galleries in London; more than a hundred paintings (there are only paintings) fill the walls of three rooms and range from rather traditional poses and formats to the experimental and even the surreal. Individual portraits, group portraits, and self-portraits are all on view — and for sale. I've twice been asked to give a public lecture about these pictures and about portraiture more generally, and I've found the experience to be both challenging and an act of provocation, for it has enabled me to extrapolate my thinking about portraiture in the eighteenth century — scattered throughout various books and essays — and apply that knowledge to works that have only recently been created. I'm now convinced that there are certain ways in which *all* portraits can (and should) be viewed, even though there are, of course, many other ways in which they can (and should) be examined as well. After considerable hemming and hawing, I have screwed up my courage (in a most un-Midwestern way) and begun to lay them down as "The Three Laws of Portraiture."

That title is obviously an exaggeration. No form or genre of painting — or of any other artistic enterprise, for that matter — actually conforms to commonly accepted laws. And even when certain laws or norms are explicitly stipulated, they are surely capable of being subverted, manipulated, or otherwise broken by any artist worth his

Sitting for One's Picture

or her salt. For several centuries, however, portrait painting in the western world has responded to an evolving series of cultural expectations: expectations about *who* might appropriately be portrayed, about *how* they might appropriately be portrayed, and about the role and status of the artist charged with the responsibility for bringing these sitters to life.

Portrait painting has its origins in religious paintings of the early modern period. Portraits of aristocratic donors — often the individuals who commissioned the work itself — were introduced at the extreme left and right sides of the painting, often in greatly reduced format. During the early Renaissance, the size and relative importance of these figures increased: increased until, little by little, the painting's donors took central stage themselves, secularizing the use of iconographic and allegorical attributes and thereby transforming the religious tradition into a humanistic one. The original purpose of the marginalized portraits was one of identity: this is who commissioned the work and this is what he or she looked like. Identity and likeness have remained at the heart of portraiture ever since, but a third factor quickly entered the equation once the sitter or sitters became the center of attention. In David Piper's clever formulation, the question of "identity" should, in successful portraiture, also include the exploration of the "entity" that lies within. It is one thing to produce a faithful likeness; it is another to reveal the character and individuality of the figure who has been depicted.

Part of the argument I've made in these talks is that the traditional focus of portraiture on likeness and character has changed very little during the modern period. It is, in fact, alive and well today no matter how radically some painters may profess to repudiate it. I enjoy introducing two examples, the first a society portrait of Beatrice Benjamin Cartwright by the Peruvian-born illustrator Reynaldo Luza. Beatrice Cartwright inherited a substantial fortune from her maternal grandfather, Henry Huttleston Rogers, one of the legendary Standard Oil magnates of America's Gilded Age. A fortune based on liquid gold supported her throughout her adventurous life, which included four husbands, numerous houses, and a swirl of parties and the jewelers

Richard Wendorf

and couturiers who pampered her. Her son, Dallas Pratt, one of the co-founders of the American Museum in Britain, remembered his mother to have been happiest when "splendidly dressed and covered with jewels, sailing into a gala occasion accompanied by an entourage — all heads turning."

This billion-dollar princess was often captured by the *paparazzi* of her era, but I find her most memorably revealed in this haughty and haunting pastel-and-gouache portrait by Luza: haunting because of the way in which her shadowy eyes suggest sadness as well as a certain detachment. Trained as an architect, Luza began his successful career as a fashion artist in New York, illustrating the sumptuous glossies of his day. Here we find him skillfully setting off what seriously mattered in Beatrice's life — those fire-engine-red lips and nails, those extraordinarily large emeralds — against the almost diaphanous nature of her clothing. The iconographic attributes have changed, but Luza presents

Sitting for One's Picture

her in the centuries-old tradition of imperial portraiture, ready at any moment to raise that elegant left hand and beckon us to her.

A similar "gesture backwards," this time rather playful, can be traced in a contemporary portrait of the art historian Roy Strong by the English painter Paul Brason, a friend who lives and works in Bath. Sir Roy is no stranger to portraiture, having served as the director of the National Portrait Gallery in London and having produced groundbreaking catalogues devoted to Tudor and Elizabethan portraiture. Brason has painted Roy Strong several times before, including a likeness in multiple perspective and a picture that associates Strong with the famous garden he has created in Herefordshire, called The Laskett. Of primary significance in this diminutive painting engagingly entitled *Small Roy Strong* is the painter's tight focus on the sitter's head, which is severed from the rest of his body as well as from any larger contextual apparatus (his clothing, his library, or his garden, for example). Everything Brason wants to tell us about Roy Strong must be captured in a very small space — measuring only 12½ by 11 inches — and without any external accoutrements. But this self-imposed restriction enables Brason to re-create the intense power of the sitter, his intelligence written all over his face (so to speak), and with Brason's brisk treatment of his hair suggesting a kinetic power that cannot entirely be restrained even within the confines of this painting. What the portrait appears to say, in fact, is that there is no such thing as a *small* Roy Strong: that would be a contradiction in terms.

Brason is quite capable of pulling out all of the iconographical stops in his portraiture, which ranges from studies of magnates and heads of Oxbridge colleges to Margaret Thatcher and the Duke of Edinburgh, whereas in this particular portrait, which enjoys such a restricted spatial format, he appears to have demurred. But "appears" is the operative word here. Consider the simple diamond stud that Sir Roy wears in his left ear. The sitter clearly wears it in order to make a statement, something along these lines: "Now that I've retired from the National Portrait Gallery and the V&A in order to cultivate my garden, I can bloody well wear and say what I want. This diamond stud is a symbol of my freedom and of the creative life I can now embrace." For Brason, moreover, the adornment of Sir Roy's ear enables the painter to associate his sitter with the many Elizabethan Englishmen whose portraits Strong analyzed and catalogued — including figures such as Shakespeare who themselves sported similar pieces of jewelry. The diamond stud is minuscule compared to the exotic emeralds worn by Beatrice Cartwright, but it places Brason and Strong in a similar tradition, one that is in fact perpetuated through their collaboration here.

These considerations of likeness, identity, and the revelation of character provide the background for my own contribution to the theory of portraiture, which is transactional in nature. My first law

Sitting for One's Picture

is that, *among the many other things it is, a portrait is always a record of the personal and artistic encounter that produced it.* The encounter I have in mind is never simply the sitting itself, important though such sittings are. Portraits often record — or at least allude to — the social and financial nature of the contract that brings the painter and the sitter together. A portrait, moreover, is sometimes the *only* record that remains of this artistic and commercial transaction, although we often have access to eyewitness accounts, correspondence, entries in the painter's account book or the sitter's journal, and even multiple portraits or several versions of the same portrait.

It is possible for artists to produce portraits of individuals who have not sat for them, or who do not know they are being observed, or who are dead — thus literally denying the possibility of an *ad vivum* likeness. But the portrait that finally emerges normally betrays the restrictions under which the artist has been forced to labor. Even when an artist's portrait is simply a copy of someone else's work — as in the many portraits of Queen Elizabeth I produced during her lifetime — the never-changing features of a monarch who refused to sit for her court painters reflect not only the putative powers of an ever-youthful queen but the remoteness of those attempting to depict her as well.

Portraits are "occasional" in the sense that they are closely tied to particular events in the lives of their subjects (a marriage, an inheritance, a new position in the community), but they are also occasional in the sense that there is usually an interval — however brief, uncomfortable, artificial, or unsatisfactory it may prove to be — in which the artist and his or her subject directly confront each other; and thus the encounter a portrait records is most tangibly the sitting itself. These sittings are social occasions as well as working sessions, and it is therefore also true, I would argue, that the relationship between artist and sitter recorded in the portrait has the capacity to suggest as strongly as any other feature the character of the individual who has been portrayed.

The sitting itself may be brief or extended, collegial or confrontational. Henri Cartier-Bresson expressed his passion for portrait photography, for instance, by characterizing it as "a duel without rules, a delicate rape." Taking a portrait, he argued, "is like a courtesy visit of fifteen to twenty minutes. You can't tie people up for a long time when you're like a mosquito that's about to bite." Metaphors such as these, violent and combative in both vehicle and tenor, contrast quite sharply with Richard Avedon's conception of a sitting: "I often feel that people come to me to be photographed as they would go to a doctor or a fortune teller — to find out how they are." Cartier-Bresson reveals himself as an interloper and opportunist whereas Avedon confesses — perhaps somewhat uncomfortably — to a role as diagnostician and (by implication) psychic healer: not as someone who necessarily transforms his subjects, but as someone who reveals their essential nature.

In the paradigm that Cartier-Bresson suggests, the artist virtually stalks his prey; in Avedon's view, on the other hand, the sitter actively searches for the artist, trusting that the therapeutic nature of the sitting, like the portrait that is eventually produced, will lead to a form of self-knowledge that has not otherwise been gained. Cartier-Bresson threatens to seize an interpretive likeness, whereas Avedon's sitters believe they will be given something in return for their cooperation. Both photographers appear to agree on one premise, however, which is that the fundamental dynamic in this process — whether successful portraiture be viewed as capturing, revealing, or transforming its subject — lies squarely in the hands of the artist. Avedon's sitters are "dependent on me," he says. "I have to engage them. Otherwise there's nothing to photograph."

A paradigm quite different from either Avedon's or Cartier-Bresson's has its roots not in confrontation or consultation but in active collaboration between the artist and his or her sitter. This very different kind of relationship ("a delicate one it is!") has been formulated most vividly by William Hazlitt in an almost entirely forgotten essay entitled "On Sitting for One's Picture," which first appeared in 1823. In addition to being an astute critic of the theater, Hazlitt was thoroughly familiar with the great English school of portraiture that extended from Van Dyck and Reynolds to the contemporary canvases of Sir Thomas Lawrence. And Hazlitt had the advantage, as well, of not only having had his picture painted several times, but of painting portraits himself during his years as an aspiring artist.

We should therefore not be surprised when Hazlitt tells us that "having one's picture painted is like the creation of another self," nor that the sitter's minute inquiries about himself during the vicissitudes (or boredom) of a sitting "may be supposed to take an indirect and laudable method of arriving at self-knowledge." What is remarkable, however, is the general principle to which Hazlitt appends these corollary truths, which is that the "bond of connection" between painter and sitter is most like the relationship between two lovers: "they are always thinking and talking of the same thing, the picture, in which their self-love finds an equal counterpart." As artist and subject reinforce and kindle each other's ardor, nothing is wanting, Hazlitt writes, "to improve and carry to its height the amicable understanding and mutual satisfaction and good-will subsisting between these two persons, so happily occupied with each other!"

The tone of this playful essay is characteristically ambivalent, for Hazlitt needs to isolate the mutual vanity of the artist and sitter while simultaneously acknowledging the benefits that may arise from it. There is a "conscious vanity" in portraiture, Hazlitt concedes, but "vanity is the *aurum potabile* in all our pleasures, the true *elixir* of human life." To illustrate his thesis, Hazlitt attempts to recapture the atmosphere in Reynolds's studio fifty years earlier:

> Sir Joshua must have had a fine time of it with his sitters. Lords, ladies, generals, authors, opera-singers, musicians, the learned and the polite, besieged his doors, and found an unfailing welcome. What a rustling of silks! What a fluttering of flounces and brocades! What a cloud of powder and perfumes! What a flow of periwigs! What an exchange of civilities and titles! What a recognition of old friendships, and an introduction of new acquaintance and sitters!

Hazlitt's point is not simply to provoke a sentimental or nostalgic impression of a world that has largely been lost. His actual focus is on the relationship — at once social, aesthetic, and financial — between a painter like Reynolds and his august clientele. It must be allowed, Hazlitt continues, "that this is the only mode in which genius can form a legitimate union with wealth and fashion. There is a secret and sufficient tie in interest and vanity." The courtier, the lady of quality, and the artist "meet and shake hands on this common ground," and it is the painter, moreover, who exercises "a sort of natural jurisdiction and dictatorial power" over the pretensions of his paying guests.

My second law of portraiture follows directly from my first, but with a twist: *among the many other things it is, a group portrait is always an exploration of the relationships between or among the figures portrayed.* If a portrait is (among other things) a representation of the encounter between painter and sitter, then that same relationship would seem to hold when the painter confronts two or more subjects in his or her studio. But group portraiture involves a change in the human dynamic of the sitting. The primary relationship is no longer that between the painter and his or her sitters (although that relationship remains in constant play), but rather between or among the sitters themselves as the painter observes their interactions and attempts to capture what he or she sees on canvas. The artist's focus is therefore bifurcated in group portraiture, resting both on the individuality of the sitters *and* on their encounter with each other.

My final law is rather different from the first two, but it is also transactional in nature: *among the many other things it is, a self-portrait is always a portrait at one remove: a representation of a representation, a reflection of a reflection.* Most of the artists who have excelled at portraiture have also taken a serious interest in painting their own portraits. One thinks immediately of Rembrandt, Van Dyck, Reynolds, Chardin, Van Gogh, and Lucian Freud. Self-portraiture provides even the youngest and least experienced painter with a ready-made sitter, and habits formed during one's apprenticeship are rarely jettisoned, given the portraitist's eye for the process of maturing and eventually for

Sitting for One's Picture

the process of aging. Joshua Reynolds's well-known early portrait of himself in oil — probably painted in 1747 or 1748 when he was 25 years old — nicely captures the intensity of this process. The artist appears to be staring directly at us, shielding his eyes from the glare of the candlelight with his left hand. In his right hand he clutches his palette, brush, and maulstick, and although he is caught in the act of painting, he is also handsomely attired, with blue silk and white linen showing beneath his brown jacket.

Reynolds's later career as a self-portraitist makes this early painting even more important, for as his self-portraits move out of the studio and into the public realm, they simultaneously lose their association with the artistic process that produced them. Reynolds was fond of saying that painting was the work of the mind as well as of the hand, and in the discourses he delivered at the Royal Academy he challenged his young listeners to aspire towards classical norms of nature and beauty. But in this early portrait the artist's hands are as conspicuous as they could be, and the powerful play of chiaroscuro suggests that the young painter had already learned a good deal from the old masters even before making his eye-opening voyage to Gibraltar and Italy.

But what, exactly, is Reynolds peering at? We could speculate that he is examining the picture he is currently painting, taking a long, close look before placing his brush and stick into play again. And if we are willing to entertain such a hypothesis, then the canvas he is staring at could be *any* of the pictures he was painting at the time. But however we decide to answer this question, we must also acknowledge that the only way Reynolds could have executed such a painting was by examining himself and his pose in a mirror — in a mirror placed in front of him together with the glare of the illuminating candle. This early self-portrait therefore serves as a vivid reminder that painters cannot directly paint themselves; they can only paint reflections of themselves (in a mirror, in a photograph, in another painting). The reflective aspect of this process therefore becomes an integral part of a self-portrait, even when it is suppressed. Every self-portrait is a representation of a representation, at one remove from the direct portrayal of other sitters.

These "laws" of portraiture have been refined and expanded over the past two decades, and I continue to sense that they stand up rather well. They certainly don't purport to tell the entire story of portraiture, but they do provide my readers (and listeners) with a mechanism for making sense of the pictures they encounter, especially when they have the opportunity to compare various paintings with one another.

Writing and lecturing on this subject is one thing, however; finding oneself engaged as part of the artistic process is quite another. In the summer of 2006 I commissioned the German photographer Thomas Kellner to create a series of images that would help us celebrate the 200th anniversary of the founding of the Boston Athenæum in 1807. Thomas's brief was to spend several weeks with us, producing not the exterior images for which he is justly famous, but rather a corpus of photographs of the interior of our landmark building, exploring both

Sitting for One's Picture

its internal architecture and the various collections it displays. Much to my surprise, Thomas decided to shoot me as well, as I sat within my office on the fourth floor of the Athenæum.

The situation was an anomalous one for both of us. Portraiture is unusual (although not unique) for Kellner to undertake because he normally shoots buildings rather than people, taking aim at a broad range of architectural targets. (The more famous the better, for there are no sacred cows within his *œuvre*.) His photographic assaults stretch from *il Colosseo* and *la Tour Eiffel* to Times Square and the Golden Gate Bridge, and at this point very few major American or European cities are innocent of his fracturing gaze. The occasion was anomalous for me because I am usually on the outside looking in, serving as the critic and historian of portraiture rather than posing as its subject. I had already advertised, through my book on Reynolds, my particular interest in the performative nature of the sitting itself, and the first of the laws of portraiture that I was honing at the time specifies, as you have seen, that, among the many other things it is, "a portrait is always a record of the personal and artistic encounter between the artist and his or her subject." But this particular sitting — *my* sitting — had taken me completely by surprise. When Thomas asked me if he could have two hours of my time, I had been focusing so intently on his work as an architectural photographer that it didn't immediately occur to me that I was supposed to spend those two hours before a camera. Where shall I pose? What should I wear? A white, summery shirt will flare in front of the lens, he cautioned me: "wear blue instead." Will my office be too small? No, we can just fit ourselves in if we move a small bench out of his way and position my chair against the bookcases instead of near my desk. May I forego my suit jacket? (It's July, after all.) No, Thomas didn't want a strong contrast between the shirt and the books behind me; the dark blue jacket will help to strengthen the composition, he says.

And so, a day later, there we were in my corner office sizing each other up. I had commissioned him, and he had now commandeered me. "How many eyes would you like to have?" he asked in his flawless, slightly accented English. Thomas's eyes are light blue and rather penetrating. He is of medium height and powerfully built, with his blonde hair tightly pulled into a ponytail. Almost every exchange brought a small smile that momentarily softened the intensity of his gaze. "Don't worry," he tells me, "you can move a bit during the first part of the sitting; I'm just going to make some notes and decide how close I should position the camera." Will he make a sketch of me, as he does in preparation for his architectural photographs? "No, I'm not really very good at drawing people." What is he doing with the little pieces of tape that he moves from his tripod to his sketchbook? "I'm determining the grid, deciding how many shots I'll take going across and how many going up. I think that you'll be a 12 by 16." A few minutes later: "No, that's too big. You'll be an 8 by 12." He really ought to have a different lens, he says, but this one will have to do. "I'm not really a trained photographer, you know."

So who, precisely, *is* Thomas Kellner? I discovered his work completely by chance several years earlier when I glimpsed three of his images in the window of the Hofer Gallery on Museum Street in London. One was of Stonehenge (that much I could make out), and another was a dizzying image of Tower Bridge; but what particularly struck my fancy was a beautiful print of an English country house, all green grass and golden limestone that appeared to have been gently imploded. My first thought was of Goethe's well-worn dictum that "architecture is frozen music." Here was a building that was enjoying — yes, "enjoying" is the right word — a slow detonation, with each piece carefully juxtaposed to its neighbors. Some were shot straight on, some with a tilt of the camera to the right, some with a tilt to the left — but all of them neatly frozen in place. What I was viewing was not a single photograph but an entire orchestration of shots, with the format of the contact sheet serving to freeze and destabilize these atomistic particles at the same time.

When I entered the gallery and expressed my interest in this particular print, the proprietor smiled as he told me that the country house in question was Lacock Abbey. And then, of course, it dawned on me that this wasn't just *any* country home but was, instead, the family estate of William Henry Fox Talbot, the progenitor of photography in England

Sitting for One's Picture

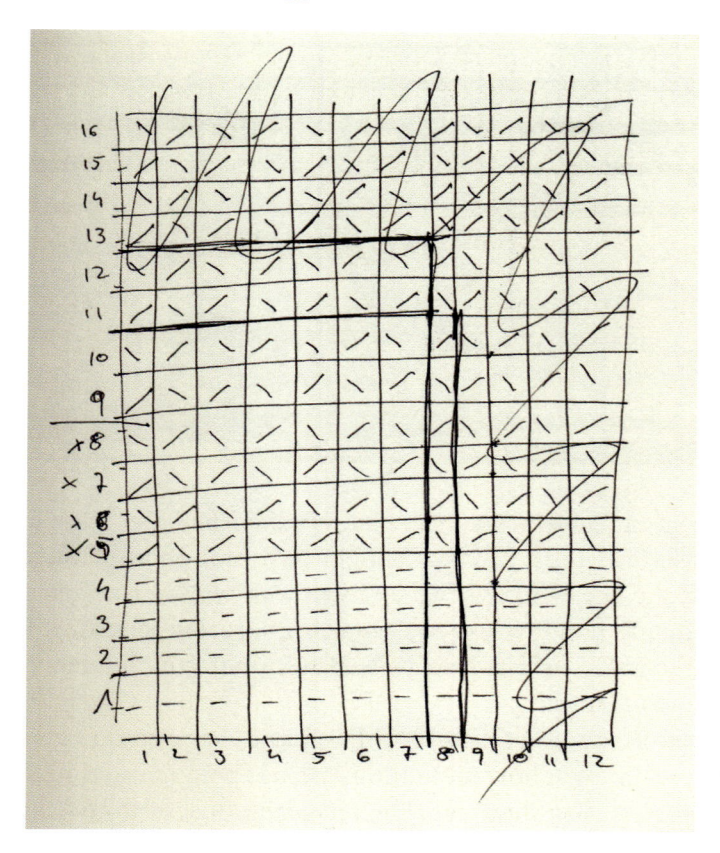

in the 1830s. This was where Fox Talbot's first experimental shots were made, and it was therefore here, deep in Wiltshire, that Thomas Kellner had brought his notebook, his camera, and his ambitious project to make us see the world anew. Kellner's image is therefore both an extended gesture of homage to Fox Talbot — a pilgrimage to one of the most important sources of photography — and an attempt to revitalize photography itself. Kellner's photographs ask us to shake off the complacency of our responses to buildings and other architectural sites that have been photographed to death by professionals and amateurs alike, to the point where these visual icons can no longer be seen in new ways. Kellner visually deconstructs a building so that we can reconstruct it ourselves, re-conceiving it both visually and intellectually. In the case of Lacock Abbey, Kellner's beautiful photograph attempts to release the powerful creative forces at work within an otherwise stable and stately home, forces that appear to break free as they begin to reshape the nature of England's visual culture during the remainder of the nineteenth century.

As I sat in my office watching Thomas as he prepared his shoot, I began to realize just how meticulously I was being placed in this grid, this formula, this *mise en scène*. The terracotta bust of Rousseau immediately to my right has moved slightly so that it's only partly within the frame; my chair has been adjusted so that the gilded frame on the eighteenth-century portrait behind my left shoulder is also fragmentary. Both of these "dis-arrangements" would be anathema to more conventional portraitists. Where, I ask, will Thomas begin? With my right knee, it turns out, for Thomas works from left to right, bottom to top, literally building up the scene. This sequence actually holds interesting benefits for the sitter, who has time to adjust to the momentum of the shoot and is therefore relaxed once Thomas reaches the head itself.

Thomas is careful to count off the number of photographs he takes in each row (8 in my case) before returning to the point of origin on the left-hand side and tilting the camera slightly upwards. At one

Sitting for One's Picture

point, perhaps in row 4, I can just make out a barely audible "oh-oh." "What's the matter?" "Oh, nothing," he replies; "I just lost my place." Does this happen often, I ask? "From time to time," he nonchalantly admits. But not very often, I imagine, for Thomas assiduously ticks off each shot in his notebook, carefully documenting the position of the camera (/ or | or \). When Thomas tilts the camera on his tripod, moreover, he puts his entire torso behind it, flexing and bending in what appears to be an intuitive rhythm: often no tilting in the external shots, tilting in opposite directions as he approaches and leaves the center of the grid. And hand-in-hand with this palpable physicality goes an intensity of *looking*: direct observation (of my knees, hands, shoulders, face) and then an alternating, even longer gaze through the lens. My strongest impression of the entire sitting, in fact, is of the intense concentration Thomas brings to the act of seeing — energy that is repeatedly turned on and off as he works his way through the entire ninety-six shots in what Susan Sontag has called the "insatiability of the photographing eye."

Energy leaves its traces. If you look carefully at one of Kellner's contact sheets, you'll notice that more *visibilia* are present than the mere sequencing of numbers. These mysterious squares and symbols — somewhat resembling a passage from a garbled electronic document — surely contain some form of coded information, but I like to think of them as the embodiment of the energy that leads from shot to shot: an electric current that hums within the bands while keeping *us* current (up to date) as we make our way through the photographic grid. It may be too much to consider this juxtaposition of images and running tag-lines as a full-fledged iconotext, but it is nevertheless the case that the signs and shapes within the broader bands play their own role as we examine Kellner's photographs either up close or from a normal viewing distance. There is visual "traffic" within the lines of the grid, a form of pulsating energy that plays with and against the inherent energy of the manipulated architectural forms themselves.

All shook up: first the building, then the viewer — or, in my case, first the sitter, then the viewer, who will have to make sense of my three eyes and meandering necktie, not to mention the hint of Jean-

Richard Wendorf

Sitting for One's Picture

Jacques Rousseau to my right and the broken portrait frame on my left. And the books, of course, are dancing, or at least flexing their buckram muscles. Is this a portrait of me or of my bookcase, I ask, as I examine my semi-detached position in the photograph? The shattered books, I notice, have begun to suggest shards of stained glass, thus reinforcing my contention that libraries and museums have become the secular cathedrals of our modern world. What is certainly true, moreover, is that the fragmentation within such a portrait produces an interesting equivalence among the assorted photographic bits. Whoever I am — or however one wishes to examine my identity — is predicated at least in part on the juxtapositions of body, clothing, statue, painting, books, and furniture. Like any portraitist, Thomas must suggest individuality through materiality; and because individuals are inevitably complex, his composite portrait forcibly argues that his representation must be so as well. "You know," Thomas says with that mischievous smile on his lips once again, "the two halves of your face are quite different from each other." Isn't that true of all people, I ask? "They're really *very* different." Is that good or bad? No answer. My hands — my hands, however — are safely locked in place, a single stable point within the surrounding swirl.

∼

I've chosen to conclude this memoir by returning to my career-long interest in portraiture and in the ways in which these images explore the character of both the artist and the sitter. My own contribution to the scholarship devoted to this genre, such as it is, has focused on the relationship between the artist and his or her subjects, between or among the sitters included in a group portrait, and between the artist and his or her encounter with their own reflected image. All of these relationships, and all of the issues associated with them, also permeate the memoir as a literary form. This particular memoir is a portrait heavily influenced by those who have helped to shape my own life and career; it is also an act of self-portraiture, which requires that unblinking encounter with the face in the mirror. Orwell famously told us that at the age of fifty we have the face we deserve. What do we make of that face at seventy (even if seventy is now the new fifty)? This book has been, among other things, an attempt to answer that question.

ACKNOWLEDGEMENTS

(And Other Conundrums)

Should there be a place for acknowledgements in a memoir? Probably not, if we consider that a memoir is, by its very nature, an extended form of acknowledgement. The act of remembering and of shaping those memories into literary form is a constant process of acknowledging those people, those texts, those works of art, and those institutions that have played a significant role in one's life — that have helped to give that life its shape and meaning. In the books I have published, I have taken pleasure (like thousands of scholars before me) in expressing my gratitude for the contributions made by friends and colleagues, even when those contributions have been rather critical: "friendly fire," one might say, and perhaps even more valuable because of those chastisements and questionings. But there is no need for such acknowledgements here. I have, I trust, thanked and cherished those friends and colleagues throughout the pages of this book — a book, moreover, that has been written very much *in solus*. No footnotes, bibliography, or scholarly acknowledgements here.

"Acknowledgement" is itself a clumsy word and in some ways an unusual one. It looks as if we began with an Anglo-Saxon verb, stretched it into a noun, slapped the French amplification of "ment" onto it, and then complicated matters even more by adding that unattractive and cacophonous "ac" as a prefix so that the word would be pronounced more or less as it had been during the medieval period. As a "token of due recognition" it works quite well in its multicultural garb, and it is one of the parts of a book that we expect to encounter — part of what Gerard Genette has called the "paratext."

But I want to continue to press on the "knowledge" in "acknowledgement," for the process of knowing in a memoir is personal, an exploration of the forces and individuals that have made such a memoir possible. Such knowledge may be faulty, of course. It may be unreliable, as Clive James conceded in the first of his own memoirs. It may be based on self-aggrandizement, on self-delusion, on the alluring temptation to be self-serving. And we mustn't forget about self-indulgence: most of us indulge ourselves in a variety of ways, and those of us who write can do so in print as well. In writing about Henry James, Adam Gopnik has argued that "the predicament of a memoir is always how to talk only about your own life without seeming to be interested only in yourself." But why is this a predicament? How can one write about one's life, one's career, one's sense of self without paying constant attention to others as well? (There are exceptions, of course, including Gore Vidal.)

To whom, finally, does one dedicate a memoir? In the past I dedicated my dissertation to my parents and my books to my partners, my brother, my children, and my closest scholarly friends. But I find myself a bit at sea here. The act of writing a memoir produces a record, at least in part, of what one has dedicated one's life to. Should one dedicate such a book to a single person? And yet we expect to see dedications in all manner of books and I, for one, am always surprised when someone has neglected to grasp the pleasure — for both the author and the dedicatee — of making such a benevolent gesture. There should be something very special indeed about a dedication, perhaps reflecting its origins in the consecration of churches and chapels. And I've also wondered why writers sometimes inscribe their books in memory of someone, a rather different gesture that means something to the author but does not allow for mutual pleasure on the part of a dedicatee. And yet — and yet — in this particular instance, having completed writing this short memoir, I think that I do see the appropriateness of naming those who are no longer with me, although they remain so in memory and in spirit: parents, friends, mentors, colleagues. *Ave atque vale.*

Credits for Images

Every effort has been made to find sources for photographs taken and images collected over a fifty-year period. Images not listed here have been taken by the author, are in the personal collection of the author and his family, or are considered to be in the public domain.

Stetson Library: John DePol, courtesy of the Chapin Library, Williams College.

Worcester College: courtesy of Conference Oxford.

Rachel Trickett: Peter Espé, by kind permission of the Principal and Fellows of St. Hugh's College, Oxford.

Houghton Library: courtesy of the Harvard College Library Communications Office.

Charles Ryskamp and Jacqueline Kennedy: Ron Galella; copyright Getty Images.

Charles Ryskamp: Richard de Liberto; copyright Richard di Liberto, The Frick Collection.

Warren Hastings: George Stubbs, courtesy of The Frick Collection.

Richard Wendorf with Josh and Toby, the Department of English, Northwestern University: Jim Ziv, courtesy of Jim Ziv/Northwestern University.

Richard Wendorf at the Houghton Library: Laura Wulf; copyright the President and Fellows of Harvard College.

James Walsh, Gore Vidal, Peter Lauritzen, and Richard Wendorf: Elizabeth Morse.

The American Museum in Britain: Chris Lacey, courtesy of the American Museum.

Yarnton Manor: Nigel Francis, courtesy of Nigel Francis Photography Ltd.

Sarah Harrop Bates: Angelica Kauffman; photograph by Justin Piperger, copyright AKRP, Bettina Baumgärtel.

20 Lansdown Crescent: Tor Gamberoni, courtesy of the artist.

Beatrice Benjamin Cartwright: Reynaldo Luza, courtesy of the American Museum.

Richard Wendorf

Small Roy Strong: Paul Brason, courtesy of the artist.

Joshua Reynolds: Sir Joshua Reynolds, courtesy of the National Portrait Gallery, London.

Sketch for photograph of Richard Wendorf: Thomas Kellner, courtesy of the artist.

Lacock Abbey: Thomas Kellner, courtesy of the artist.

Richard Wendorf in 96 photographs: Thomas Kellner, courtesy of the artist.

Richard Wendorf at the American Museum (*author photograph on back flap*): Leon Day, courtesy of Leon Day Images.

INDEX

Achebe, Chinua, 100
Allen, Brian, 67
American Museum in Britain, 117-131 *passim*
Amherst College, 23
Amory, Hugh, 95
Antonioni, Michelangelo, 32
Archer, Richard, 29
Armstrong, Rodney, 112
Arnold, Eddy, 11-12
Arnold, Matthew, 36
Art Institute of Chicago, 150
Aubrey, John, 66
Auchincloss, Andrew, 115-116
Austen, Howard, 114
Autry, Gene, 12
Avedon, Richard, 172

Bain, Joseph and Carol, 110, 113
Baird, John, 49
Bakhtin, Mikhail, 100
Balanchine, George, 26
Barkan, Leonard, 64, 151, 152
Baroque (and Rococo), 61-62, 66
Bartrum, Barry, 48
Bate, Walter Jackson, 55, 105
Bates, Sarah Harrop, 148-150
Bath (England), 132-142 *passim*, 152-162 *passim*
Bath Royal Literary and Scientific Institution, 132
Bath Spa Hotel, 134, 153
Bath Spa University, 109
Baumgärtel, Bettina, 150
Baxandall, Michael, 65
Beaton, Cecil, 52
Beckford, William, 154-161
Beinecke Library, 71, 92, 97

Belanger, Terry, 90, 102
Benjamin, Walter, 87
Bentinck-Smith, William, 106
Berek, Peter, 27
Bernstein, Leonard, 110
Biography and portraiture, 65-66, 166-184
Blake, William, 58, 63
Bloom, Harold, 49
Boston, 33, 94-95
Boston Athenæum, 33, 35, 97, 110-131 *passim*, 176-178
Boswell, James, 44, 65
Bourdieu, Pierre, 1
Brason, Paul, 169-170
Brettell, Richard, 150
Bromwell family (cousins), 7-8
Burden, Carter, 110-111
Burney, Frances, 44-45
Butler, Samuel, 35

Calapai, Letterio, 76-78
Cambridge Scientific Club, 55
Cameron, David, 136
Carter, Matthew, 129
Cartier-Bresson, Henri, 171-172
Cartwright, Beatrice Benjamin, 167-169
Cedar Rapids, Iowa: 3-23; public library, 16-17; *Gazette*, 18; 143-145
Chapin Library (Williams College), 28-29, 42
Chaucer, Geoffrey, 29
Chicago, 6, 10, 33, 73, 94-95, 146-150, 152
Chicago Merchandise Mart, 146-147
Clark Art Institute, 63, 66

Clark, T. J., 65
Collins, William, 42, 50-58 *passim*, 65, 70
Compton Verney, 119-120
Country music, 11-12
Cowper, William, 49

Dennis, Rodney, 104
Díaz, Dr. Paul, 21
Diebold, Richard, 110
Disraeli, Benjamin, 140
Dodsley, Robert, 51
Donne, John, 26
Dryden, John, 26, 40
Dvořák, Antonin, 3

Elizabeth I, Queen, 171
Emin, Tracey, 137, 138

Faison, Lane, 63
Feng, Y. T., 94
Finney, Michael, 86
First Presbyterian Church, 15-16
Fisher, Frederick, 37-38
Fleeman, David, 41
Forster, E. M., 27
Fort, Bernadette, 64
Foxon, David, 41-43
Franks, Lord, of Headington, 35
French, Diana (second wife), 146, 162
Frick Collection, 52, 56, 59
Fried, Michael, 65

Galella, Ron, 52
Gardner, Dame Helen, 43
Garfield, James, 30
Garvey, Eleanor, 106-107
Gaudino, Robert, 25
Gearin-Tosh, Michael, 41
Gee, David, 78-79

Genette, Gerard, 185
Gere, Richard, 144
Gifford, Don, 29
Gillray, William, 77
Goethe, Johann Wolfgang von, 178
Goodkin, Michael and Helen, 90
Gopnik, Adam, 186
Gore, Albert, 63
Graver, Lawrence, 26-27

Hamilton, Sir William, 78-79, 159-160
Hagstrum, Jean Howard, 63-64
Hastings, Warren, 59
Hazlitt, William, 172-174
Hill, Barbara Hilderman (first wife), 53, 146, 162
Hilles, Frederick W., 71
Hitchcock, Sir Alfred, 32
Hofer Gallery, 178
Hogarth, William, 61-62, 73-74, 77, 146
Holden, Robert, 150
Hollenbeck, Donald T., 22-23
Hopkins, Mark, 31, 32
Horblit, Harrison and Jean, 108-109
Houghton Library, 90-110, 114-131 *passim*
Hubacek, Richard, 21-22
Hunt, James Clay, 25-26
Huntington Library, 65-66, 100, 118
Hyde, Mary, Viscountess Eccles, 55, 110, 111

Iowa: *see* Cedar Rapids

Jackson, William Alexander, 28, 100, 104-106
James, Clive, 1, 185
James, Henry, 186
Johnson, E. J., 63

Index

Johnson, Samuel, 40-41, 55, 65
Johnson, Stanley, 73-76, 79, 81
Joyce, James, 10, 29

Katz, Stanley, 101
Kauffman, Angelica, 148-151, 158
Keats, John, 63, 104-106
Kellner, Thomas, 176-183
Kennedy, Jacqueline, 52-53
Killian Department Store, 13-14, 17
King, James, 49
Krüger, Hardy, 135

Lacock Abbey, 178-180
Lambert, Grace Lansing, 53-55, 146
Lauritzen, Peter, 114
Lees-Milne, James, 155
Legman, G., 135
Leslie Hindman Auctioneers, 147-148
Levine, James, 58
Library of Congress, 110
Lind, Michael, 116
Lipking, Lawrence, 48, 50, 64
Lonsdale, Roger, 41, 43, 51, 154
Losey, Joseph, 135
Louvre, 120
Luza, Reynaldo, 167-168

Marie de France, 38, 46
Martin, John Rupert, 61-63, 65
Matisse, Pierre, 110
Maylone, Russell, 76
McCormick, Col. and Mrs. Robert, 148-149
McLaverty, James, 42
Mehta, Ved, 33-35
Mellon, Paul, 52
Mellon, Rachel (Bunny), 50, 52
Memoir (nature of), 1-2, 183-186
Mendez, Christopher, 80

Michelangelo, 26
Michener, James, 143
Midgley, the Rev. Graham, 39-41, 43
Miller, Henry Knight, 48
Milton, John, 26, 163
Miner, Earl, 48
Mitchell, W. J. T., 70
Monroe, Marilyn, 119, 127
Morgan Library, Pierpont, 49, 52, 56, 59, 100, 110-111
Morris, Leslie, 115
Morris, William, 29
Morse, Elizabeth (third wife), 35, 162
Museum of Fine Arts (Boston), 121

Naipaul, Sir Vidia, 100-101, 111
Najm, Sami, 24, 32
National Portrait Gallery (London), 169-170
Newberry Library, 100
New Yorker, The, 18, 142
Nochlin, Linda, 65
Nordel, Joan, 109
Northwestern University, 63-65
Nyhan, David, 95

Olsen, Larry, 21
Oxford, University of: see Worcester College

Parissien, Steven, 119-120
Paul Mellon Centre, 67
Paulson, Ronald, 64, 67
Phi Beta Kappa, 14
Pierson, William, 63
Piper, Sir David, 167
Piranesi, Francesco, 75, 80
Piranesi, Giambattista, 70, 73-89, 158, 159
Pollock, Griselda, 65
Pope, Alexander, 41, 42

Portraiture: *see* Biography and portraiture
Pottle, Frederick, 49
Pratt, Dr. Dallas, 168
Praz, Mario, 161
Pressler, Frank, 7
Pressler, Maurine Hamblin (aunt), 4-16 *passim*
Princeton University, 48-57, 61-63, 134-135

Ransom Center, Harry, 92
Rare book and manuscript libraries, 90-103
Redwood Library and Athenæum, 118
Rembrandt van Rijn, 74-75
Reynolds, Sir Joshua, 67, 71-72, 77, 173-176
Rheault, Charles, 107
Richardson, Samuel, 40-41
Ricoeur, Paul, 1
Roach, Joseph, 75
Roberts, David Gainsborough, 119
Robison, Andrew, 85, 86
Rogers, Henry Huttleston, 167
Rohe, Mies van der, 146
Rosenthal, Angela, 150
Rosenthal, Robert, 90-91
Rossetti, Dante Gabriel, 70
Roworth, Wendy, 150
Royal Society of Portrait Painters, 166
Rudenstine, Neil and Angelica, 111
Ryskamp, Charles, 48-60, 63, 88, 145, 146

Samuels, Charles Thomas, 31-32
Saturday Club (Boston), 55
Scottsdale, Arizona, 18-19
Seattle, 7

Seiden, Melvin, 107
Sistine Chapel, 121
Smith, Carl, 64
Sontag, Susan, 181
Soyinka, Wole, 100
Steiner, Wendy, 70
Stern, David, 25
Stoddard, Roger, 77, 109
Stoddard, Whitney, 63
Stoddart, Frances, 158
Strong, Sir Roy, 169-170
Stubbs, George, 59
Suffolk University, 113
Swift, Jonathan, 40

Talbot, William Henry, 178-179
Trickett, Rachel, 43-46
Trinity College, 23
Turner, Bob and Gloria, 146-147
Turner, Michael, 90
Twycross, Meg, 37-38, 41, 43

Valadier, Hotel, 22
Van Dyck, Anthony, 66
Verba, Sidney, 94, 110
Vidal, Gore, 113-116, 186

Walsh, James, 114-116
Walton, Izaak, 66
Wark, Robert, 65
Washington Senior High School, George, 20-23
Weingartner, Rudolph H., 65
Weinreb, Ben, 80
Wendorf, Harold (father), 3-24, 143-144
Wendorf, James (brother), 4-23 *passim*, 35
Wendorf, Jeanne Hamblin (mother), 3-24, 143
Wendorf, Richard: childhood, 3-19;

Index

stamp collecting, 9-10; high school, 20-23; public speaking, 21; undergraduate years at Williams College, 23-32; graduate program at Worcester College, Oxford, 33-47; graduate program at Princeton University, 48-57; relationship with Charles Ryskamp, 48-59; transition from English literature to British art history, 61-72; collecting Piranesi, 73-89; directorship of the Houghton Library, 90-103; development work at the Houghton Library and the Boston Athenæum, 104-116, 122-123; comparative experience as a library and museum director, 117-131; living in England, 132-142; collecting and interior design, 143-165; recent work as a novelist, 163-165; laws of portraiture and as the subject of a portrait, 166-184

Wendorf, Richard, publications: *The Works of William Collins*, 50-51, 57-58; *William Collins and Eighteenth-Century English Poetry*, 65, 68; *The Elements of Life*, 66-67, 68; *Sir Joshua Reynolds*, 67, 68; *After Sir Joshua*, 67, 68, 70; *The Scholar-Librarian*, 69; *The Literature of Collecting*, 69; *Director's Choice: The American Museum in Britain*, 69; *The Three Laws of Portraiture*, 69, 166-176; *Abandoning the Capital* (in progress), 70-71; *Rare Book and Manuscript Libraries in the Twenty-First Century* (ed.), 98, 123; *America's Membership Libraries* (ed.), 124, 126; *The Boston Athenæum: Bicentennial Essays* (ed.), 124, 126

Whitcroft, Michael and Sandie, 153
Wilde, Oscar, 132
Wilders, Dr. John, 35-37, 40, 43
Wildi, Liz Hopkinson, 162
Williams College, 14, 23-32, 63
Willson, Meredith, 3
Winckelmann, Johann, 88
Windsor, Duke of, 56
Winterthur Museum, 117
Wolff, Christoph, 110
Wood, Grant, 3, 6, 20
Worcester College, Oxford, 33-47

Yale Center for British Art, 58, 71-72
Yarnton Manor, 145
Yourcenar, Marguerite, 75

∼

I thank the following friends and colleagues for their kind assistance in providing images for this book: Bettina Baumgärtel; Paul Brason; Matthew Brown (Conference Oxford); Penelope Currier (The Frick Collection); Leon Day; Nigel Francis; Wayne Hammond (Chapin Library, Williams College); Kate Hebert; Susan Hill; William Humphreys; Amanda Ingram (St. Hugh's College, Oxford); Thomas Kellner; Leslie Morris (Houghton Library); Katie Nash (Williams College Archives and Special Collections); Cherie Rogers; Nada Samuels; Julie Vane Watts; David Webb; Laura Wulf; and Jim Ziv.

And I warmly thank Scott Vile for designing this book – our ninth venture together – and Matthew Young and the late (and much-revered) Robert Fleck for what is now my fourth collaboration with Oak Knoll Press.

∼